MINI

Patrick C. Paternie

MOTORBOOKS

Dedication

This book is dedicated to Paddy Hopkirk,
who can still show you the proper way to drive a Mini, old or new.
He also sets a fine example for getting the most out of life.

First published in 2002 by Motorbooks, an imprint of MBI Publishing Company, Galtier Plaza, Suite 200, 380 Jackson Street, St. Paul, MN 55101-3885 USA

© Patrick Paternie, 2002

Motorbooks titles are also available at discounts in bulk quantity for industrial or sales-promotional use. For details write to Special Sales Manager at MBI Publishing Company, Galtier Plaza, Suite 200, 380 Jackson Street, St. Paul, MN 55101-3885 USA

ISBN 0-7603-1157-9

On the front cover: A MINI Cooper at the base of San Francisco's Golden Gate Bridge. *MINI USA*

On the frontispiece: Short overhangs, wheels at the corners, wheel spats, and discrete chrome accents bring "Mini-ness" to the new MINI. *MINI USA*

On the title page: This MINI Cooper poses with another icon of the transportation world, the San Francisco cable car. *MINI USA*

On the back cover, left: This MINI Ride is not set up to accept money, but it does represent one of many unique marketing gimmicks employed to sell the MINI. *MINI USA*. **Right:** The MINI is a nearly perfect urban car–small, easily maneuvered, and stylish. *MINI USA*

Edited by Peter Bodensteiner
Designed by LeAnn Kuhlmann

Printed in China

CONTENTS

ACKNOWLEDGMENTS

Although you only see the author's name listed on the title page, there are a lot more people who contribute in various ways to get a book written and published. First and foremost, I would like to express gratitude to my editor Peter Bodensteiner and MBI Vice President Zack Miller for the patience, direction, and redirection they supplied regarding my efforts in writing this book.

My thanks to the people at MINI USA who were able to take some time from their focus on launching the MINI into the U.S. market to provide access to the information, photos, and vehicles used in preparing this book. Jack Pitney deserves a nod for his ability to conduct an in-depth interview regarding the MINI marketing plans while serving as navigator on a long test drive that included some spirited nose-to-tail running on a twisty forest road and a passing maneuver that probed the far side of the MINI's big, round, centrally located speedometer.

Special thanks go to Martina Martes, Corporate Communications Manager at the Oxford MINI factory. Martina graciously provided me with a comprehensive plant tour on relatively short notice. The information and materials she supplied during my visit to Oxford were most valuable.

Other people I would like to thank include Mitch Rossi and Joe Rusz for supplying photography, and Matt Stone for a compilation of historical information. Peter Cameron at Special Vehicle Concepts (SVC) kindly gave me free rein in driving his modified Cooper S. Don Racine and the people at Mini Mania also provided time and information regarding their efforts at race-modifying the MINI.

As usual thanks to my wife, Linda, who puts up with all the grumbling and strange work habits that are essential parts of my writing *modus operandi*. My appreciation and gratitude also extend to anyone else who had to put up with my whining, ranting, and raving (much of it with good cause, as you know) during the writing of this book.

INTRODUCTION

The appeal of the MINI Cooper, at least for those of us who classify ourselves as car enthusiasts, is that it delivers on the performance and fun promised by its styling. This makes the MINI more than just a fad or fashion statement, setting it apart from other nostalgia-based vehicles such as the first wave of PT Cruisers or new Beetles. It is a car that you can enjoy driving even after the trendies move on to something else.

Of course, emulating the personality and performance characteristics of its predecessor plays a big part in the MINI's allure. What red-blooded car crazy hasn't fantasized about zipping down a flight of steps or through a culvert after watching Minis perform those stunts in *The Italian Job*? Just as outrageous and inspiring were the real-life adventures of drivers like Paddy Hopkirk, slithering through snow- and ice-covered mountain roads while holding off the challenges of Porsches and Ferraris.

My first encounter with a Mini was at an MG Club driving school at Nelson Ledges racetrack in the early seventies. I decided that the guy driving a Mini seemed to be fairly knowledgeable about race driving, so I followed him in my MGB, determined to learn the nuances of going fast on the track. After 20 minutes of flailing about trying to keep pace behind the Mini, I was flagged in by my instructor who asked me what exactly I was trying to do out on the course. When I told him that I was trying to emulate the Mini, the instructor offered his advice. It was meant in reference to what was then the peculiarity of front-wheel drive, but was nonetheless descriptive, of many other things Mini. "Never follow a Mini," he said. "They do weird things."

Let's hope that the MINI can follow the Mini and carry on doing those weird things.

The changing of the guard. Although the original Mini survived more than four decades and sold more than 5 million copies around the world, even hardcore Mini maniacs had to agree that it was time for a more modern successor. The taller, wider, longer MINI is still one of the smallest new cars on the market. The disc brake rotors on the new car, however, are larger than the 10-inch wheels of the old one. MINI USA

Chapter One

A MINI HISTORY:

Britain's Best

The original Mini may have been short in physical stature but it was long in history. Production of the 10-foot-long car spanned 41 years. The first cars rolled into the world on August 26, 1959. By the time production ceased in October 2000, 5.3 million Minis had been manufactured. It remains the best-selling British car of all time.

The Mini was runner-up to Henry Ford's original "better idea," the Model T, in voting by a panel of 130 international automotive journalists assembled in 1999 to elect a "Car of the (20th) Century." Not bad when you consider that the Mini never really made much of a sales impression in the country that has the world's largest appetite for automobiles. Fewer than 10,000 Minis were officially sold in the United States from 1960 to 1967. Gasoline was cheap and a brand new interstate highway system promised high-speed, traffic-free access to the New Frontier, so Americans were more interested in muscle cars and land yachts than an economical little shoebox on tiny 10-inch wheels. It wasn't, however, the response of U.S. consumers as much as the U.S. government that finally killed off Mini sales in the states. The increasing cost of meeting emissions and safety regulations became too much to justify for a car with such a—wait for it—mini-sized sales potential.

Bubble Bursting

The Mini found a much different climate in England. In 1956, British support of Israel against Egypt's nationalization of the Suez Canal led to gasoline rationing in the United Kingdom. In response to this fuel shortage, British motorists

Top: The motivating force behind the development of the Mini for BMC was the influx of micro cars from Germany and Italy following of the fuel crisis caused by British involvement in the dispute over ownership of the Suez Canal. Cars like this German Goggomobil were little more than motor scooters with automotive bodywork.

Above: Sir Alec Issigonis poses with a pair of Morris Minis. Given a free hand to develop a small car for the masses by Leonard Lord, chairman of the British Motor Corporation, Issigonis combined his earlier experiments in front-wheel drive with his obsession to pack the maximum amount of people and cargo into a minimum amount of space. The outcome was a car that would set the standard for compact sedans still followed a half century later. *MINI USA*

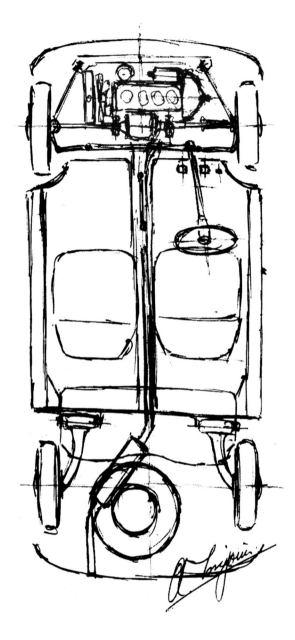

Issigonis was famous for sketching out his thoughts on whatever was handy, including cigarette pack wrappers and tablecloths. These drawings were then handed over to his small staff, including Jack Daniels and suspension genius Alex Moulton, for fine-tuning. *MINI USA*

turned to driving imports with engines under 300ccs, like the Isetta and Messerchmitt. These were not so much automobiles as they were motor scooters with extra wheels and enclosed bodies. Distinguished by bulbous styling and relatively large windows (some Messerchmitts had aircraft-style cockpit canopies) in proportion to their tiny overall size, these cars came to be known as "bubble cars."

Leonard Lord, the chairman of the British Motor Corporation (BMC) at the time, decided that his company needed to come up with a small but practical car to blow the bubble cars off the highways. He assigned the task of designing such a car to a somewhat eccentric engineer by the name of Alec Issigonis.

Issigonis loathed the idea of using market research to design cars. He also felt anything beyond the bare necessities, including a radio, was a distraction for the driver. The free-thinking Issigonis felt that the ideal automobile packed the maximum amount of passengers and cargo into the minimum amount of space. In 1948, Issigonis demonstrated that philosophy and an understanding of the needs of British automobile buyers when he conceived the Morris Minor, the first British car to exceed one million production units. Lord intended to play off this success by having Issigonis come up with a smaller variant to become known as the Morris Mini-Minor.

Lord's confidence in him gave Issigonis a free hand to do as he saw fit, with the only stipulation being that an existing BMC engine had to be used to power the new car. Issigonis had already experimented with a front-drive version of the Minor in 1952. That car also featured a transverse-mounted engine. Fifty years later this has become common practice in small-car design, but at the time Issigonis definitely was thinking out of the box. Actually, he was thinking "in the box" because his idea for the Mini was to create a car shaped like a box that was 10 feet long, 4 feet high,

needs of a 1,300-pound car when it was packed with four people and their luggage. Alex Moulton, who would also earn notoriety for his innovative work involving bicycles with diminutive wheels, was the man behind the Mini's rubber suspension. Later models of the Mini would feature Moulton's ingenious Hydrolastic suspension.

Other examples of Issigonis' zealous commitment to maximizing the Mini's internal space were the use of sliding plastic side windows so that the doors could be as thin as possible, and a trunk lid that dropped down to serve as a shelf.

The engine chosen for the Mini was BMC's four-cylinder A-series, which had a displacement of 848cc and put out 34 brake horsepower.

To make things even more compact up front, the engine and gearbox shared the same oil sump. In order to simplify the Mini's construction, external welds joined the body panels. The door hinges were also exposed. This allowed cheaper, less skilled workers to assemble the cars. Mounting the engine/transmission, steering, and front suspension to a separate subframe that was then attached to the main body also simplified the manufacturing process. Likewise, a subframe was also used in mounting the rear suspension. More importantly, the use of subframes provided an additional buffer that kept noise, vibration, and harshness from either the engine or the road surface from being transferred to the passenger

and 4 feet wide. By mounting the engine sideways with the transmission mounted underneath, he could use 80 percent of his "box" to haul people and their luggage.

Having done away with the drive shaft tunnel, Issigonis went even further to maximize interior space by making other mechanical components less intrusive. He determined that the Mini's wheels should be placed at the vehicle's extreme corners and limited in size to 10 inches. The use of a rubber-cone suspension took up less room than a more traditional spring and shock setup. It was also better able to cope with the weight-bearing cabin. The Mini was also innovative in finding new ways to use established parts or ideas. The A-series powerplant was the most obvious example. Less obvious were the c.v. joints that transferred the engine's power to the Mini's front-wheel drive system. They were supplied by Hardy Spicer and based on those used in the 1930s-era Cord 810/812.

Many Minis

Issigonis was able to go from rough sketches to a prototype for Lord to test-drive in 15 months. Lord's drive took place in 1958 and the BMC chairman was so impressed he ordered Issigonis to have the Mini in production within a year. Because BMC was formed in 1952 by a merger between the U.K.'s two largest automakers,

Nuffield (Morris, MG, Riley, and Wolseley) and Austin, two versions of Issigonis' new design were to be manufactured. These were the Morris Mini-Minor, which was built at the Cowley plant, and its identical twin (save for name badges), the Austin Seven (or Se7en), manufactured in Longbridge. On August 26, 1959, both factories rolled out their respective versions of what would become a British motoring icon.

It would not be until British icons like Peter Sellers and the Beatles began driving customized versions that the Mini would achieve its own icon status. At first sales were slow, the first year's production reaching only about 20,000 cars. It didn't take too long, however, for the Mini's ingenuity and personality to be discovered, ironically by affluent jet setters and other trendy types

Issigonis completed his engineering studies at Battersea Polytechnic in London but not before failing math three times. He later declared that mathematics was "the enemy of every truly creative man." It was his disdain for rigid rules that led him to stray from conventional automotive design by mounting the Mini's engine sideways and powering the front wheels to gain more space for people and luggage. Issigonis, who passed away in 1988, is often quoted as stating, "A camel is a horse designed by a committee." *MINI USA*

before its intended working-class audience caught on. By 1962, production was up to 200,000 cars a year and would stay at that level for the next 15 years.

In 1961, other divisions of BMC received versions of the Mini. These involved more than simple badge engineering, however. The Wolseley Hornet and Riley Elf were Minis hiding behind a façade of front-end styling awkwardly downsized and grafted on in hopes of creating a resemblance to their adopted families. Further damage to the Mini's simple lines was carried out at the rear, where Wolseley and Riley added bustle-like trunk appendages to increase luggage space. As befitting their intended upscale customers, these variations also had more luxurious interiors with wood trim, something that rankled Issigonis' sense of simplicity.

Cooper Calls

A less compromised and more exciting version of the Mini also appeared in 1961, one that would play a major role in turning the Mini into a success story. This version was the Mini Cooper.

If the Mini was initially a slow mover off the showroom floor, it was just the opposite at the racetrack and in rallies. An Austin Seven was entered in the Norwegian Viking Rally only one month after production began in 1959. This initial outing resulted in an ignominious 51st place overall. One month later, at the British national rally with an event title that proved both prophetic and propitious, Pat Moss and Stuart Turner drove a Morris Mini-Minor to its maiden victory in the Mini Miglia.

One of the early production cars used in the press launch, Austin Seven A-A257/589—registered as YOK 250—was loaned to racecar builder John Cooper in September 1959 for evaluation. Cooper's Formula One car, driven by Sir Jack Brabham, was on its way to both the drivers' and manufacturers' F1 world championships in 1959. Brabham and Cooper would repeat this feat in 1960. Cooper was also the first British company to build a car to compete in the Formula Junior series that debuted in 1959. Class rules limited engine size to one liter. Cooper chose the BMC A-series as the basis for his race engine.

Cooper was also interested in producing a high-performance road car. He had experimented with the rear-engined Renault Dauphine, but after driving the Mini he immediately was impressed with the greater potential of its front-wheel drive and transverse-mounted engine. Unfortunately, Issigonis did not share his enthusiasm and

The Incredible Austin Se7en, and its almost identical sibling the Morris Mini-Minor, were considered family transport suitable for four adults. Austin and Morris had been combined to form BMC, but retained separate manufacturing facilities and product lines. Austin manufactured most of the 10,000 cars that came to America before importation ceased in 1967. In 1962, the Austin Seven name was officially changed to Austin Mini. *MINI USA*

Despite being designed as a "people's car" intended to provide low-cost transportation to the masses, the Mini was not an immediate success. It wasn't until celebrities, like Ringo Starr and the other Beatles, as well as wealthy "jet setters" began driving the cars that the general public got caught up in Mini madness. *MINI USA*

reacted petulantly to the idea of his concept for a "people's car" being converted into a sports car. Nevertheless, Cooper built a modified Mini with an engine tuned to Formula Junior specs that reportedly had 100 horsepower. He also installed a pair of prototype 7-inch Lockheed disc brakes up front. The work was completed in two weeks.

Ignoring Issigonis, Cooper took his prototype Mini to the head of BMC, George Harriman, who had succeeded Leonard Lord. A brief drive was all that was necessary for Harriman to commit to an initial run of 1,000 Mini Coopers. BMC would pay Cooper a royalty of £2 per car. A handshake sealed the deal.

The cars were to be built at the Austin factory in Longbridge under a new BMC project number, ADO 50, as opposed to that of the standard Mini, which was ADO 15. Working with the BMC engineering staff, Cooper determined the modifications that would transform an Austin or Morris Mini into an Austin or Morris Mini Cooper. As opposed to the peaky, high-compression (11.5:1), race-prepped 994cc engine used in the Mini Cooper prototype, the standard Mini 848cc would be retained because of its low-end torque. It was calculated that in order to achieve a top speed of 85 mph, the engine would have to produce 55 brake horsepower. To achieve this, the stroke of the 848cc unit was lengthened from 76.2 mm to 81.28 mm while the bore dropped slightly in size from 62.94 mm to 62.43 mm. This resulted in a displacement of 997cc, conveniently under the 1.0-liter limit for competition purposes. Other modifications from the standard Mini engine included two 1.25-inch SU HS2 carburetors, larger intake valves, revised cam timing, and a higher (9.0:1 versus 8.3:1) compression ratio. These changes combined to make the 55 brake horsepower at 6,000 rpm and 54.5 ft-lb of torque at 3,600 rpm. To cope with the increased power output, the block and cylinder head were

MINIS IN AMERICA

The Mini may have been in the right place at the right time for the British market, but a number of factors were working against its success in the United States. Only 10,000 Minis officially came ashore in the U.S. from 1960 through 1967 before the British Leyland company, a 1968 merger between BMC and Leyland, decided to pull the plug rather than devote time and money to meet the ever-increasing emissions and safety regulations.

When the Minis first began to trickle into U.S. showrooms in 1960, British makes were well represented in the United States. The distribution network for BMC products such as MG, Austin-Healey, Morris, Riley, and Austin consisted of over 1,000 dealers. British cars were still riding the wave of the postwar sports car boom when 90 percent of the cars imported to America came from England. Unfortunately, it was a downhill ride caused by reliability problems, notably the vagaries of the Lucas electrical systems and product engineering that failed to take into account the effects of the more extreme climate variations in the U.S. By 1967, these issues, coupled with the Volkswagen Beetle's low price and solid German engineering, had tipped the import scales. British cars accounted for only 10 percent of the market they once dominated.

Ironically, it was the sports car crowd that eventually was responsible for whatever limited sales success the Mini did achieve. The racing exploits of the Mini Cooper and Cooper S in Sports Car Club of America (SCCA) road races and rallies soon made it a favorite of those drivers who appreciated a pint-sized family sedan that could run rings around bigger cars, even sports cars. The Mini Cooper became known as a Q-ship, a name adopted from the cleverly disguised vessels used by the German navy during World War II. Posing as harmless freighters, the Q-ships would lure their prey in close before launching a devastating attack with their hidden weapons.

Today the Mini leads a dual life in American racing as a popular competitor in SCCA production-class racing against newer cars as well as being a favorite among the vintage racing set.

The Mini may never have enjoyed a broad mass-market appeal in the U.S., but those that know it must love it. How else can you explain that 10,000 Minis were officially imported by BMC from 1960 to 1967, but today there are about 12,000 Minis in the U.S?

strengthened and a crankshaft damper and stiffer valve springs were added.

The transmission featured close-ratio gears but final drive remained at 3.765:1. A shift lever extension made for sportier gear changes.

Suspension and wheels remained as stock but the 7-inch front disc brakes of the prototype were also fitted to the production Mini Cooper along with 5.20-10 high-performance Dunlop Gold Seal tires.

Externally, there was not a lot to distinguish a Cooper from its more plebian counterpart. Aside from Cooper badges on the hood and trunk, a more stylish radiator grille was added to the Cooper models. This grille was further distinguished by the use of seven horizontal slats on the Morris version and 11 horizontal slats on the Austin. The Cooper bumpers featured full-length bumper guards and overriders, front and rear. Almost all the Mini Coopers had two-tone paint schemes, with the roof painted white or black in contrast with the body. For 1961 models only, a gray roof could be ordered with either a green or white body.

The interior of the Cooper was much more opulent in contrast to the Spartan surroundings of the standard Mini. The carpeting was plusher and sound insulation was thicker. The seats and door panels were done up in two-tone color schemes with a gold or silver brocade cloth available on cars with certain external colors. A carpeted "boot shelf" hid the spare tire and battery located in the trunk. Besides chrome plating on the gearshift lever and the steering column bracket, the driver also viewed an oval-shaped instrument binnacle containing three instruments. A large, round 100-mph speedometer with an integrated fuel gauge occupied the center and was flanked by two smaller gauges: one on the left indicating water temperature, and the other, on the right, showing oil pressure. A key start ignition switch

replaced the floor-mounted start button of the basic Mini.

Production of the Mini Cooper began on July 11, 1961, and the car made its official debut on September 20 of that year. Also debuting about the same time were versions of the Mini that offered the interior and exterior equipment and two-tone paint schemes of the Cooper without any performance modifications. These "luxury" models were sold as the Morris Mini-Minor Super and the Austin Super Seven. They would devolve (losing the two-tone paint and Cooper interior trim) a year later to become the Super Deluxe, the top of the standard Mini lineup.

By the end of 1961, 1,775 Mini Coopers were built, 912 of those wearing Austin badges. In 1962, production increased dramatically to 13,964 cars, with the Austin version again being slightly more popular at 7,159 units.

Super Cooper

In April 1963, the Mini Cooper S debuted. The car was primarily designed to provide maximum performance while conforming to the rules of the Group 1 class of international motorsports. The engine was a less high-strung version of the 1,100cc A-series engine used by the Cooper Formula Junior racecars. The bore of the race motor was decreased from 71.6 mm to 70.64, while the standard stroke of 68.3 mm was retained to produce a displacement of 1,071cc. This allowed the larger valves and stronger cylinder heads of the race motor to be retained. Compression was 9.0:1. The race motor put out 98 brake horsepower and revved to 7,800 rpm. The Cooper S engine made 70 brake horsepower at 6,200 rpm but with a flat torque curve stretching from 2,500 rpm all the way to 5,500 rpm that was ideal for high-performance street duty. The Cooper S modifications were good for an amazing 4-second drop (to 13 seconds) in 0-to-60-mph time over the 997cc Mini Cooper. Top speed also went up to 95 mph.

The Cooper "S" debuted in 1963 with an engine that broke the 1-liter barrier for the Mini. The 1071cc S powerplant put out 70 horsepower at 6,200 rpm and had options like 4.5-inch wheels and a close-ratio gearbox. What really made the Cooper S legendary was a top speed of 95 mph and the ability to scamper from 0 to 60 mph in 13 seconds—not bad for any sedan before the muscle car era. *MINI USA*

Besides the larger engine, the Cooper S was fitted with front brake discs that measured 7.5 inches in diameter as well as being slightly thicker. Dunlop SP radials (145-10) were an option as were 4.5-inch wide wheels. An oil cooler and auxiliary fuel tank were also optional. Inside, the only change was the substitution of a 120-mph speedometer.

Evolution

January 1964 saw a change in the engine compartment of the base model Mini Cooper. Although engine size only increased from 997cc to 998cc and horsepower remained at 55 brake horsepower, the results were much more dramatic. This new version of the A-series engine had a stroke of 76.2 mm and a bore of 64.58 mm to improve torque from 54.5 ft-lb at 3,600 rpm to 57 ft-lb at 3,000 rpm. Top speed increased to almost 90 mph and acceleration time from 0 to 60 mph came down from over 17 seconds to under 15 seconds.

Another big change in 1964 was the switch in September to Alex Moulton's Hydrolastic suspension. The system consisted of pressurized fluid-filled bags at each wheel. Hoses connected the front bag to the rear bag on either side of the car so that as one wheel traveled over a bump it

MINI-CYCLOPEDIA

Total number produced:	5,387,862 in 133 versions including convertibles, pickups, and station wagons.
Selling price, UK, 1959:	£495 ($1,275)
Selling price, UK, 1999:	£10,000 ($15,000)
Selling price, USA, 1960:	$1,295 ($1,675)
Horsepower, 1959:	34 brake horsepower
Horsepower, 1999:	64 brake horsepower
Some famous owners:	The Beatles, Peter Sellers, Peter Ustinov, David Bowie, Mick Jagger, Kate Moss, Princess Margaret, Lord Snowdon, and Twiggy. Swinging sixties clothing designer Mary Quant was so taken with her Mini that she named her revolutionary high-hemmed skirt after it.
Most People in a Mini:	On August 25, 1999, to celebrate the Mini's 40th anniversary, 25 people jammed themselves inside a Mini to set a world record.
Most Famous Movie Role:	Climbing stairways and racing through sewers as getaway cars used by a gang of gold thieves in the 1969 cult classic, *The Italian Job*, starring Michael Caine.

compressed the bag, which transferred pressure to the other bag. The main advantage of this self-damping system was a more comfortable ride and the elimination of shock absorbers. Despite this, racing Minis either retained the old tried-and-true rubber-cone suspension or ran with the hoses of the Hydrolastic system blocked off. Although the system was known to spring a leak now and then, the Hydrolastic suspension was phased out beginning in 1969 primarily because of its higher cost. It remained on the Cooper S until 1971.

Two more variations of the Mini Cooper S also came out in 1964. A short-stroke 970cc engine model was available primarily for racing purposes. The high-revving engine put out 65 brake horsepower at 6,500 rpm and was offered for less than a year. Quite the opposite was a larger 1275cc engine that would effectively be the basic powerplant of all subsequent versions of the Mini Cooper. Because of the performance

improvements derived from the larger engine, the 1071cc Cooper S was discontinued in August 1964. Top speed for a 1275cc-powered Mini was now 97 mph, while 60 mph could be reached from a standing start in 11 seconds.

The Mini Cooper S was responsible for the Mini's most famous competition win, when Paddy Hopkirk drove one to victory in the grueling 1964 Monte Carlo Rally. Proving it was no fluke, a Cooper S repeated the feat a year later, this time in the hands of Timo Makinen. A three-peat for Mini at the Monte was nullified in 1966 when French officials disqualified the Mini Coopers that had finished one-two-three. The Minis supposedly had lighting systems that did not comply with the rules. A French car, a Citroen DS 19 driven by Pauli Toivonen, was handed the win. It only took a year for the Mini Cooper to get its revenge. Rauno Aaltonen, the third BMC factory driver, drove his Cooper S to a win in the 1967 Monte.

19

The debut of the sporty Cooper version in July 1961, developed by racer John Cooper, and its subsequent motorsports victories were major factors toward increasing public interest in the Mini. A major event in Mini history was when Paddy Hopkirk and co-driver Henry Liddon won the grueling 1964 Monte Carlo Rally, beating more powerful sports cars. *MINI USA*

Mark II

In October 1967, after 1.6 million versions of the original Mini had been produced, the Mark II version of the Mini and its Mini Cooper siblings debuted. Changes were slight. From the outside, the second edition featured a squared-off grille, wider rear window glass, and larger, rectangular-shaped tail lamps. Inside, the trim and carpet were upgraded but color choice was limited to black. A multi-function stalk controlling the horn and headlight dimmer was mounted on the steering column. Mechanical improvements included a new steering rack that decreased the turning circle radius from 37 feet to 28 feet. The Cooper's slicker-acting shift lever, minus its chrome plating, trickled down to the more mundane Minis. The 998cc Mini Cooper got a fully synchronized gearbox in October 1968, as did the Mini Cooper S.

BMC merged with Leyland in early 1968 to become British Leyland under the chairmanship of Donald Stokes. Stokes set out to streamline operations in 1969 by dropping the Riley and Wolseley versions of the Mini. Henceforth, the Austin and Morris prefixes would also be dropped and the car would simply be called the Mini. The 998cc Mini Cooper was also history. The Mini Clubman, with a lower-spec, single-carburetor 38-bhp version of the 998cc A-series powerplant, replaced it.

Mark III

The Mini lineup, including the Cooper S, received a major facelift in 1970 as the external door hinges were eliminated and wind-up windows were installed. The last Mini Cooper S was produced in June 1971 when the original royalty agreement with John Cooper expired. Only 1,570 of the Mark III Cooper S were manufactured. In all, about

Classic Mini production ceased in October 2000. John Cooper died shortly thereafter on December 24, 2000. He and his son Mike were both involved in the development of the new MINI Cooper. The John Cooper works in England offers high-performance parts for both the old and new cars. *MINI USA*

108,000 Mini Coopers were made during a 10-year lifespan. Of these, around 27,000 were S versions.

Epilogue

The Mini Cooper would continue to be produced under a separate agreement between John Cooper and the Innocenti brothers, a small manufacturer of specialist vehicles who built high performance Mini variants, until 1976. The basic Mini would survive until October 2000.

This "old" Mini displays several of the classic cues that have been passed along to the new MINI, including bonnet stripes, contrasting-color side mirrors and roof, and the chrome grille and bumper. MINI USA

Key elements that bring "Mini-ness" to the look of the MINI were short front and rear overhangs, placement of the wheels at each corner, the addition of wheel spats, and discrete chrome trim accents around the lights and door handles. The idea was to look evolutionary, not retro. *MINI USA*

Chapter Two

DEVELOPING AND DESIGNING THE NEW MINI:

The Mini Becomes the MINI

The design and development of the original Mini was basically a one-man show produced and directed by Sir Alec Issigonis. He sketched out the initial concept, managed the small but dedicated and talented development team that included Alex Moulton and Jack Daniels, and later got John Cooper involved. Clearly, Alec Issigonis was the father and motivating force behind the original Mini.

It is just as clear that the Mini's nationality was British. It originated as a weapon of "home defense" put forth by England's auto industry in response to the invasion of imported "bubble cars".

Four decades later, the development of the new MINI reflects the changes that have occurred in the automobile industry and the world since its namesake debuted. There is neither a single individual nor country that can lay claim to its creation. While the old Mini was a British car with a quirky design and personality that developed a worldwide cult following, the new MINI has international roots, being a product of Germany's Bavarian Motor Works, and its design follows the intent of being a world car. The other major difference is that the original Mini's aim was to provide cheap, efficient, and economical transportation for the masses. The new MINI, while remaining true to its predecessor's penchant for providing space efficiency and economy of operation at a low price, is also aimed at customers looking for a higher level of performance and luxury as well.

It is a bit ironic that the man in charge of designing the follow-up to this very British motoring icon was an American, Frank Stephenson. Stephenson was actually born in Morocco and raised in Europe before attending college in California. *MINI USA*

Gert Volker Hildebrand, the man in charge of the MINI Design Team for BMW, explains that the concept driving the design of the new MINI was "to create a full-fledged four-seater inspiring and thrilling the customer in the new millennium and thus extending far beyond short-lived fashion trends. The car was to embody the joy of life, bringing different classes, countries, and generations together."

Hildebrand reports to Chris Bangle, Design Director of the BMW Group. The seven-person MINI design team included Frank Stephenson, the chief designer of the MINI, Marcus Syring, handling interior design, and Marisol Manso Cortina, responsible for color and trim. In 2001, they relocated to a separate design center around the corner from the BMW Research and Engineering Center in Munich. The design of the production MINI that debuted at the 2000 Paris Motor Show, however, owed its development to Stephenson and a more diverse group of designers than the current team.

BMW Take Charge

BMW became involved with the new Mini, renamed MINI once BMW decided to make it a separate brand under the BMW Group, when it acquired the Rover Group in 1995. At the time, the old Mini was still in production, but Rover had begun planning to develop its successor. This work was being carried out in England at the Rover design center in Gaydon.

The idea within BMW of producing a car similar to the Mini did not, however, start at this time. BMW had been conceptualizing the idea of a new small car since the early 1990s. Therefore, the company's management understood the potential of the new MINI to expand the BMW brand into the small car market. BMW's Dr. Norbert Reithofer, Member of the Board of Management–Production, has explained the MINI as an entry-level model that will appeal

TALE OF THE TAPE: Mini á MINI

	2002 MINI COOPER	1961 Mini
No. of doors/seats	3 / 4	2 / 4
Vehicle length	142.8	120.25
Vehicle width	66.5	55.5
Vehicle height	55.4	53.0
Wheelbase	97.1	80
Track front/rear	57.4 / 57.7	48.5 / 46.0
Unladen weight	2,315	1,315
Gross vehicle weight	3,263 / 948	2,004
Engine	Transverse mounted SOHC Inline 4-cylinder 4-valves per cylinder	Transverse mounted OHV Inline 4-cylinder 2-valves per cylinder
Fuel management system	Siemens EMS 2000	Two SU HS2 Carburetors
Displacement	1.6 liters (1598cc)	1.0 liter (997cc)
Stroke/Bore-inches	3.37/3.03	3.20/2.46
Horsepower	115 at 6,000 rpm	55 at 6,000 rpm
Maximum torque	110 at 4,500 rpm	54.5 at 3,600 rpm
Compression ratio	10.6:1	9:1
Transmission type	5-speed all synchromesh	4-speed synchromesh top 3 gears
Final drive ratio	3.94	3.765
Steering type	Rack and Pinion with Electro-Hydraulic assist	Rack and Pinion
Brake front/diameter	Vented Disc 10.9 inches	Vented Disc 7.0 inches
Brake rear/diameter	Disc 10.2 inches	Drum 7.0 inches
Top speed - mph	124	85
Acceleration 0-60 mph	8.5 seconds	17 seconds
Standing quarter-mile	16.6 seconds	21 seconds
Fuel consumption city/highway	26/43 mpg	27/35 mpg
Front suspension	MacPherson struts, coil springs, tube shocks, anti-roll bar	Independent with unequal length transverse links, rubber springs, hydraulic telescopic shocks
Rear suspension	Multi-link, coil springs, tube shocks, antiroll bar telescopic shocks	Independent with trailing arms, rubber springs, hydraulic
Tire size/type	175/65R15/Radial	5.20-10/Bias-ply
Wheel size/type	5.5x15-inches alloy	3.5x10-inches steel

to a new group of customers at prices well below those of the BMW 3-series. He also sees MINI production being a way for BMW to meet environmental commitments by lowering the overall average carbon dioxide emissions of its entire sales fleet. He does not however, envision the front-wheel drive MINI taking sales away from the future rear-drive BMW 1-series that should be priced somewhere between the MINI and the 3-series.

"The MINI Cooper is a genuine MINI, not a BMW," says Reithofer. To Reithofer the MINI is a way to tap into the entry-level luxury market niche from which MINI buyers would someday move up into more expensive BMW models.

Dr. Burkhard Goschel, development director of the BMW Group, said that only the technical package of the MINI had been settled when BMW took over Rover. Although the Rover design team at Gaydon continued to advance on the actual design of the car after its acquisition, BMW also opened up the project to its people in Munich and a California subsidiary, Designworks, as well as an outside design firm. When it came time to choose a final design, the review involved 15 full-size models submitted by these various sources. The winning design was the one submitted by BMW's Frank Stephenson. Stephenson is an American with a degree in automotive design from California's Art Center College of Design. His design was selected because it achieved the middle ground in a spectrum of concepts that went from little more than a freshening of the old Mini to what the Rover team called the Spiritual, an ovoid, rear-engined hatchback and its minivan sibling, dubbed the Spiritual Too.

"Mini is a central element in the story of the automobile," Stephenson said. "For the brand's new products, our mission was to combine the emotional power of the original model with the technology of the future."

"The MINI Cooper is not a retro design car, but an evolution of the original," declared Stephenson when the inevitable question of how much the old Mini influenced the look of the new MINI. "It has the genes and many of the key characteristics of its predecessor, but it is larger, more powerful, more muscular, and more exciting than its predecessor ever was."

Hildebrand stated that the goal was to "follow as far as possible the original design" in terms of the original Mini's short overhangs and efficient packaging. Like Stephenson, he also stressed that the MINI is not a retro car but that it is "an evolution from one original to the next."

Stephenson's version of the MINI first appeared in public as a concept car displayed at the 1997 Frankfurt auto show. Three years of development and one major change in the development team took place before the production version took the stage at the 2000 Paris auto show.

Gearing Up For Production

Until March 2000, development of the new Mini was carried out in England by the Rover development center in Gaydon. Coinciding with this was the establishment of the Mini production facilities at Rover's Longbridge manufacturing plant in Birmingham. When BMW decided to divest itself of the Rover group but hold on to the Mini project, quick action was called for in establishing a new development team as well as shifting the location of the manufacturing plant.

Dr. Heinrich Petra was responsible for establishing the new project team for the MINI at BMW's Research and Engineering Center in Munich. He also had to oversee the relocation of the Mini production line from Longbridge to Oxford in exchange for the Rover 75 line at the latter location. (See chapter 4.)

Petra currently has about 70 people working for his MINI team, about 70 more than he had when he first took on the MINI project for BMW

FRANK STEPHENSON

The chief designer of the MINI was born October 1959 in Morocco. He attended high school in Madrid. His college education included completion of the Bachelor of Arts program at Pasadena City College in Pasadena, California, before transferring to the Art Center College of Design, also in Pasadena, where he was awarded a Bachelor of Science in Automotive Design degree in 1986.

Stephenson worked on concept design projects for General Motors in 1985 at the Cadillac and Corvette Advanced Design Studios in Warren, Michigan. From 1986 to 1991 he was employed by Ford, where he worked on exterior and interior design at Ford Werke AG in Cologne, Germany, and on concept vehicles at Ghia in Turin, Italy. Stephenson has also been an instructor at the Art Center College of Design in Pforzheim, Germany, and in Geneva, Switzerland.

In 1991, he worked at BMW AG in Munich on design work for automobiles and motorcycles. Since 1996, he has been with the BMW Group working on the MINI at Gaydon and now Munich.

Stephenson became the MINI's design chief after his concept was selected from a field of 15 finalists. It first appeared as a concept car at the 1997 Frankfurt auto show. His job was to carefully balance a blend of the old Mini characteristics with new features while avoiding the curse of the "retro look." MINI USA

---

in June 2000. Although all of the British Mini project team were offered positions in Munich, only two decided to make the move. The rest chose to remain in England and take up positions with either MG Rover or Ford-owned Land Rover.

"In about two and a half weeks, thanks to considerable support from the directors and divisional managers, we had managed to get a new team together. They didn't know each other, they had never worked together, and they were faced with an entirely new task. We were thrown in the deep end," Dr. Petra recalls. "It didn't take

long for the team to learn to swim. We were 100 percent operational within 30 days."

With production of the MINI scheduled to begin in April 2001, Petra's quickly assembled team faced the dual tasks of getting the Oxford plant switched over from Rover 75 to MINI manufacturing and reorienting the MINI's product development process to comply with the standards prescribed by BMW corporate policy. The latter task meant that despite what had been done by their Rover predecessors, Petra's people had to perform a complete evaluation of the MINI

Left: The MINI was designed and developed the "old-fashioned way," using a full-scale clay model. Many of today's designers choose to make smaller scale models to check the actual three-dimension proportions against what appears on the computer screen. They consider the "old school" method too time-consuming. *MINI USA*

Below: It was important for the new car to have a Mini "face." A mesh grille was deemed too aggressive, so a modernized version of the traditional Mini slats was used. Separate round turn signals also won out over more radical streamlined units. Hood stripes and the checkerboard roof graphic are options that pay homage to the racy Cooper S.

covering everything from ride and handling to crash testing, comfort, and appearance.

Because deadlines could not be postponed and there was no slack in terms of meeting BMW's corporate guidelines, it was important that decisions be made quickly and with a minimum of red tape. Petra worked closely with Oxford plant manager Dr. Herbert Diess to quickly solve any problems, including issues of quality control and supplier relationships.

Petra gives credit to the MINI suppliers for their cooperation with Diess and himself. "They were quick to understand what BMW standards imply, including the speed required, and they put their backs into it," Petra said of the suppliers who would meet at the factory every other Saturday to review quality issues.

One of the innovations that Petra and Diess employed to speed up development time was the use of aluminum tooling for pre-production models. Aluminum tooling can be made much quicker than traditional steel tooling, but without sacrificing the quality of its output. This meant that changes and modifications to parts could also be done more quickly. The drawback of aluminum tooling is that its wear rate makes it impractical for use in regular production.

Actual production of the MINI involves a number of diagnostic programs and tests to ensure that components do not stray from the expected norms and any quality control issues that arise with suppliers can be quickly settled.

Commenting on the production launch, Dr. Diess said: "The MINI has met all the stringent BMW pre-production quality targets and as a result we are able to start producing cars for dealers and their customers on schedule."

In 10 months, Petra and his MINI team went from nearly a start-up operation to full production. There is no time, however, for them to sit back and enjoy the laurels of successfully bringing the world a new MINI.

As in the original, a transverse-mounted, four-cylinder engine drives the front wheels, allowing the MINI to be the shortest car on the market. A big battle won by the design team was the approval of a huge one-piece hood that includes the headlights. The piece is difficult to fabricate, but Stephenson and his team felt that the smooth, rounded look of the MINI would be compromised if broken up by shut lines on a smaller, more conventional hood arrangement. *MINI USA*

"We are already heavily involved in the development of new model versions, including a diesel version," noted Petra. He added that "modifications and optimizations" will be as much a part of the MINI production process as continuous reviews of quality control and cost-saving analyses.

The Art of MINI-ness

Frank Stephenson has stated, "The key thing in designing the new MINI was to capture the spirit of its predecessor, but in a modern-looking design."

The most obvious trait inherited by the new MINI is the wheel at each corner that Alec

The rear of the MINI presents another area where design won out over manufacturing ease. Stephenson felt that individually mounted taillights were a characteristic of the original Mini that needed to be part of the new car. Modern manufacturing calls for the taillights to be mounted on the edge of the trunk opening to save time and money. Concealed roof pillars also create the effect of the lid-like top on the original. *MINI USA*

Issigonis pioneered to maximize space efficiency and provide outstanding handling and road holding. Stephenson suggests looking beyond the overall proportions of his design to the details that also play an important role in adding a Mini-esque appeal to the new car.

Starting at the front of the car, Stephenson points to the round headlamps with round turn indicators below them that ensure that the new MINI's "face" is clearly recognizable as a Mini.

During the design process, a more radical approach was tried that involved mounting the indicators in the A-pillars, but some of the familiar look was lost. Different versions of the front grille were also tried, including one with a sporty mesh insert. This was deemed too aggressive for the MINI's overall personality. In the end, it was decided to go with a modernized version of the classic Mini slatted grille, split by the front bumper.

At the rear, ease of production came in second to what Stephenson refers to as "Mini-ness" when choosing the tail lamp treatment. "Minis always had tail lamps set away from the shut lines (the gap between the body and trunk) and we were keen to carry this over," he said, despite the fact that modern cars feature tail lamps flush with the shut line to simplify manufacturing.

Above: The interior of the MINI follows the same basic principles laid down by Issigonis in 1959. Rear seats are designed to hold full-size adults comfortably for more than a ride around the block. *MINI USA*

Left: One of the key interior design elements is the centrally mounted speedometer. A more modern central "pod" was tried, but discarded as being too "space age." Another throwback to old British cars of the 1950s and '60s is the use of toggle switches mounted on the dash to operate lights and other accessories. They disappeared as safety officials deemed them hazardous to occupants in case of an accident. The relentless Stephenson came up with unique chrome "safety bars" so the new MINI could have controls as cool as the old one. *MINI USA*

The new MINI follows the lead of its predecessor in terms of style and function. Contrasting colored roof and mirrors (available in black or white) are similar to the color scheme of old Coopers, as is the option of choosing white as opposed to silver wheels. *MINI USA*

When it came to top off the MINI, the shape of the roof satisfied both the aesthetic aspirations and the necessary modern practicality. The original car featured a lid-like top that has been emulated in the new car by concealing the roof pillars behind the glass. The practical benefits are additional headroom along with a spacious, airy interior.

More Mini-ness comes from the decision to use add-on spats around the wheel arches instead of contouring the fenders to cover the oversize wheels and tires that are integral to the sporty handling and attitude of the new MINI. Many early Minis wore these add-on spats, and Stephenson

chose to make the new ones a contrasting color to the bodywork to enhance their custom flair.

One last element that Stephenson felt was a key ingredient in the appearance of both the old and new Minis was chrome. The chromed door handles and bezels surrounding the head and tail lamps are carried over to the MINI. Also available as an option are chrome inserts for the bumpers.

Inside the MINI, the idea was "to create a surprising and up-to-date driving environment, but one that still clearly reflects the car's heritage," said Stephenson. This was achieved by using toggle switches, a staple on British sports cars of the '50s and '60s, in place of more conventional knobs and buttons to operate fog lights and power windows. "Eyeball" air vents are reminiscent of the type found on later versions of the original Mini. The large, round speedometer centrally located in the dash was inspired by the one featured on Minis through 1968. Early design sketches enclosed the speedometer in a central pod that was deemed too "space age" for the MINI.

The two-spoke steering wheel used in the early Minis was emulated, albeit updated and housing an air bag, of course, rather than going with a sportier three-spoke racing-style wheel. Also brought up to date are the inside door panels. Large openings made best use of the space available in the old Mini and the new MINI follows suit. The satin finish tubing that is used as trim on the center console and on the door panels is meant to recall the roll cage bracing of early racing Minis.

Of course, the new MINI can boast its own original styling features. The one that Stephenson is proudest of is the large one-piece engine cover that encompasses almost the entire front end including the fenders, headlights, and upper portion of the grille. There are no seams or joints to interrupt the lines of the car's front end. Stephenson admits that engineering and manufacturing such a large body part was difficult, but the engineers and production people enthusiastically cooperated in order to achieve the style and quality intended.

A much simpler solution provided the MINI's sporty classic-looking exhaust tip. Stephenson and his crew had been working around the clock to finish up the full-sized clay model of the new MINI in time for a presentation to the board of directors. They finished with a few hours to spare, which prompted Stephenson to declare a hard-earned beer break to celebrate. That's when he spotted the problem.

The clay model was lacking an exhaust tip. Inspiration struck when Stephenson got the idea

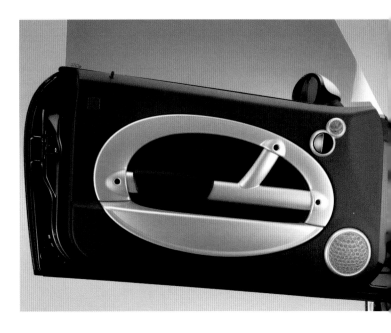

A good example of a modern interpretation of an original Mini theme can be found in the door panels. The first Minis omitted wind-up windows so that extra storage space could be had inside the doors. The new MINI has deep storage areas as well, even with power windows, while the armrest and handles are tubular to emulate the roll cage of a racing Mini. *MINI USA*

to strip the paint off his beer can, punch out a hole in it, and stick it in the clay at the appropriate spot.

"The review went off without a hitch," Stephenson recalls. "The board told me not to change a thing. Imagine the difficulty I had communicating the specifications of the exhaust to the supplier without telling him to go copy the sides and bottom of a beer can."

Stephenson eventually confessed upon being chastised by management for wasting the valuable time of the modeler who had to mill the exhaust piece. Fortunately, after the initial stunned silence, his confession was greeted with the hearty laughter that it deserved.

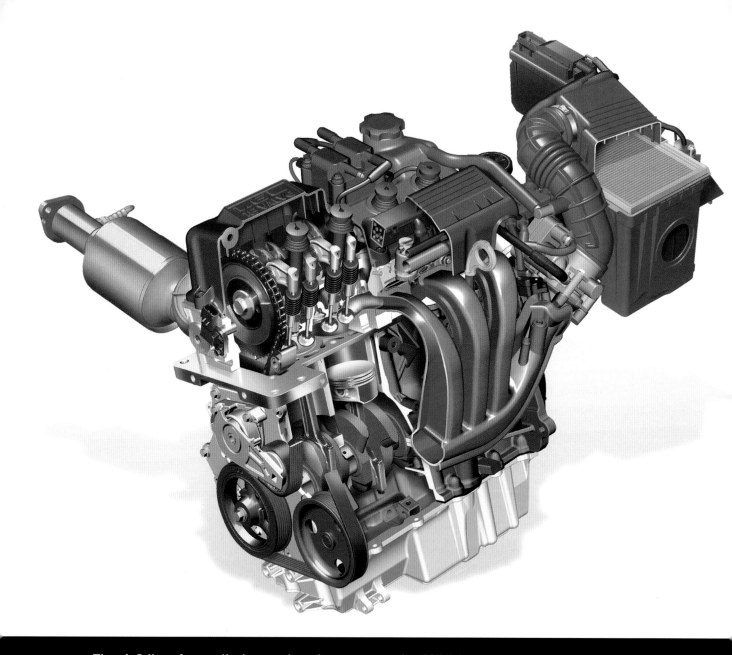

The 1.6-liter four-cylinder engine that powers the MINI is a Chrysler design that is built in Brazil by Tritec, a joint venture between DaimlerChrysler and BMW. The engine was designed in Detroit for use in overseas versions of Neons and PT Cruisers. It has a chain-driven overhead cam and four valves per cylinder. *MINI USA*

MINI MECHANICALS:

Under the Skin

Technically, the United States does not get a MINI, only MINI Coopers – the 115-horsepower MINI-Cooper and the supercharged 163-horsepower MINI Cooper S. The base model MINI, called a MINI One, is not sold in the United States. A bit more Spartan but still nicely equipped and appointed, with basically the same engine and mechanicals, the MINI One gives up some performance for better fuel mileage, a trade-off most American buyers would be loath to make until U.S. fuel prices match those in Europe. Comparing the U.K. versions of the MINI One and the MINI Cooper, the MINI One has 25 less horsepower (90 versus 115) and weighs 20 pounds less to eke out about 5 percent better fuel mileage. It also has a slower speed (115 mph versus 124 mph) and takes 1.7 seconds longer, 10.9 seconds total, to hit 62 mph (100 km/h). That is significantly quicker than the original Mini Cooper, but more like a minivan than a Mini Cooper in the eyes of today's U.S. small car performance buffs.

The MINI Motor

Just as the original Mini used an existing BMC powerplant, the new MINI fills its engine compartment with a 1.6-liter motor, versions of

This side view of the MINI engine illustrates its compact size. It was designed to leave space for "crush zones" to safely handle the impact of a collision. Note how the alternator is attached directly to the block. *MINI USA*

which can also be found in non-U.S. editions of the Dodge Neon and PT Cruiser. This engine is manufactured by Tritec Motors Ltda., a 50/50 joint venture between the BMW Group and DaimlerChrysler. Tritec is located in Brazil. The name is derived from the fact that three countries —Germany, the United States, and Brazil—were all involved in its establishment. The joint venture was formed before Mercedes-Benz became involved with Chrysler.

The Tritec plant cost about $500 million to build. Its construction began in April 1998, and by September 1999 it commenced engine production. Current plant capacity is 250,000 engines a year with a capability to expand to 400,000 units a year.

Tritec is located at Campo Largo, which is near Curitiba, Brazil. The Curitiba area is home to a number of other automotive manufacturers and suppliers including Volvo, Bosch, and Siemens. Audi, Renault, and Dana have also recently established facilities in Curitiba. The high concentration of auto-related firms in the locale is evidenced by the fact that 75 percent of the material content of the Tritec engines comes from Brazilian suppliers, with a target of increasing that number to 90 percent by 2003.

The 450,000-square-foot Tritec facility is completely state of the art. Its workforce consists of about 300 employees who report to a joint management team of BMW and Daimler-Chrysler executives. The major components of the engine—the block, cylinder heads, crankshaft, and connecting rods—are all produced on-site. Despite being a joint venture with another automaker, Tritec is fully integrated into the BMW manufacturing network as a part of the BMW engine and chassis business unit.

Chrysler engineers in Michigan designed the 1.6-liter inline four-cylinder unit, referred to as the "Pentagon" engine. It features a cast-iron block, five main bearings, and a chain-driven

Cooper S versus Cooper. The hood scoop and more aggressive front bumper treatment of the Cooper S (on left) are easy to spot in this picture. The Cooper S has the standard 16-inch, V-spoke alloy wheels while the standard Cooper wears its standard seven-hole, 15-inch alloy wheels. Also shown are matching colors for the mirror and roof, available on either model in black or white. *MINI USA*

single-overhead camshaft with a 16-valve cast-aluminum head. The bore measures 77 mm and the stroke is 85.8 mm for a displacement of 1,598cc. The engine was specifically designed as a transverse power unit with the transmission, water pump, and air conditioning compressor attached directly to the engine block for maximum utilization of the available engine compartment space, thereby providing the space necessary for crash impact "crush zones."

A "drive-by-wire" electronic throttle (BMW calls it "E-Gas") transmits the driver's urges to a Siemens EMS 2000 multipoint fuel injection and engine management system. Cooper S models augment this setup with an intercooled, mechanically driven (by a toothed belt off the crankshaft) Roots-type supercharger that operates at up to 0.8 bar of boost. An external oil cooler and internal oil squirters for cooling the pistons are also additions to the 163-horsepower S version of the engine. Other "S" modifications affect the exhaust system,

valves, crankshaft, cooling system, and engine management parameters.

The normally aspirated Cooper engine has a 10.6:1 compression ratio versus the 8.3:1 ratio of its blown S counterpart. Maximum torque for the 115 bhp Cooper is 110 ft-lb at 4,500 rpm, while the torquier S makes 155 ft-lb at 4,000 rpm. Top speed is electronically limited to 124 mph on the Cooper and 135 mph for the Cooper S. Active knock control allows for the use of unleaded fuel ranging in octane from 87 to 98, although premium grade 91-octane unleaded fuel is recommended for peak performance.

BMW's decision to use the Tritec engine in the MINI was borne out of expediency and its low cost of manufacture. A 1.6-liter diesel alternative for European models, probably a joint venture with Toyota, is rumored to be in the works. Also anticipated are gasoline engines in which BMW engineers will be more directly involved in the design and development.

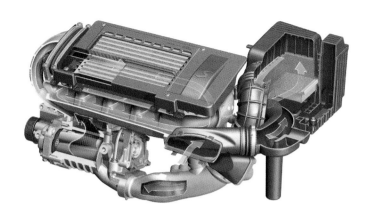

The key to the tremendous power increase from the 1.6-liter Pentagon motor enjoyed by the Cooper S over its MINI Cooper sibling is a Roots-type supercharger. Running off the crankshaft rather than exhaust gases as with a turbocharger, the supercharger does not need time to "spool up" to start making horsepower. Consequently there is no turbo lag. An intercooler cools down the compressed (and thus, heated) intake charge for additional power. *MINI USA*

The CVT (continuously variable transmission) can be used in a set-it-and-forget-it automatic mode or, on sporting occasions be manually shifted through a set of six predetermined ratios which BMW refers to as "steps." Six LEDs on the speedometer let the driver know which step he or she is in. *MINI USA*

Transmissions

Three transmissions are available on U.S. MINI Coopers. A close-ratio five-speed manual comes standard on the Cooper. It is a two-shaft unit, code-named R65, that has seen use over the years in a number of Rover front-drive vehicles. Its roots can be traced to a Peugeot-Citroen design. Like the Tritec engine, expediency played a role in its use for the MINI Cooper. The gearbox is manufactured in Longbridge, but BMW retained its rights to the gearbox when it divested itself of the Rover Group.

The high-powered Cooper S, on the other hand, comes with a newly developed and more robust three-shaft six-speed manual transmission from BMW's traditional gearbox supplier, Getrag.

Optional equipment on the MINI Cooper is a CVT (continuously variable transmission) automatic transmission. The CVT has two major advantages over a conventional automatic transmission. First, it is physically smaller and lighter, and second (but first from the driver's perspective), it is more responsive. A CVT-equipped

MINI Cooper only weighs 33 more pounds (2,557 pounds versus 2,524 pounds, unladen) than its 5-speed counterpart. The MINI Cooper CVT replaces the traditional torque converter with an oil-bath multi-disc coupling that is electronically controlled by the engine management system to transmit engine output to the front wheels. The transmission itself consists of a fixed-length steel drive belt moving along a pair of pulleys that are cone-shaped so as to provide infinitely variable transmission ratios. The position of the pulleys is electronically monitored so as to continually provide the optimum ratio for driving conditions.

The CVT also features a "Sport" mode that can be selected to provide ratios more suited to high-performance driving. There is also a Steptronic feature that allows the driver to manually select, by moving the gear lever forward or back, from a range of six predetermined ratios, or steps, that emulate the gears of a traditional transmission.

Suspension

The underpinnings of the MINI rely more on the wide "wheel at each corner" stance, the extremely rigid body structure, and judicious fine-tuning than technological innovation to provide what BMW describes as "Go-Kart-like handling." The front suspension, to save weight and space, is a familiar strut layout consisting of MacPherson struts, coil springs, tube shocks, and an anti-roll bar. Equal-length drive shafts are used to deliver

This view of the MINI chassis gives a better perspective of how the body's short overhangs just barely cover the suspension without any wasted space. Wheels shown are the optional (for the MINI Cooper) 16x6.5-inch, five-spoke alloys with all-season run-flat 195/55R-16 tires. *MINI USA*

power to the front wheels in order to reduce torque steer.

The multi-link rear suspension derives from the patented multi-link Z-axle rear setup used in BMW's 3-series cars since the 1980s. It has been re-engineered to fit the space requirements underneath the smaller MINI so as not to compromise trunk space or rear seat room. Coil springs, tube shocks, and an anti-roll bar are also part of the rear multi-link arrangement.

The Sport Suspension Plus that comes standard on the Cooper S has firmer springs and stiffer anti-roll bars than those on the MINI Cooper. The setup, however, is available as an extra-cost option on the less powerful model.

The Cooper S comes with traction control as standard equipment. This system uses the ABS sensors to detect wheel slippage and cuts power to any spinning wheel until traction is regained. The driver may switch off this system.

A more advanced form of traction control, dynamic stability control (DSC), is an option available on both the Cooper and Cooper S. DSC monitors lateral and longitudinal forces on the vehicle and wheel slippage, as well as throttle and steering inputs. Sometimes referred to a "yaw

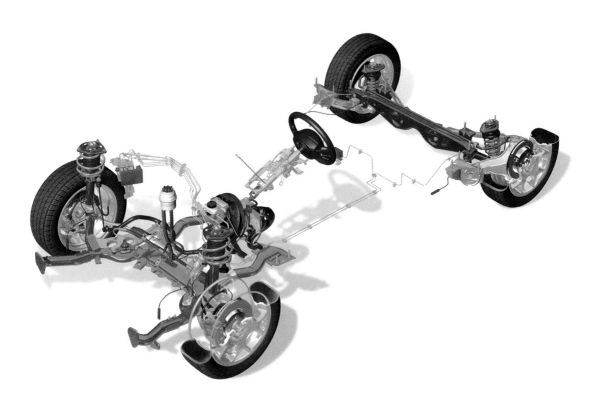

The MINI's underpinnings are a combination of simplicity and high technology. Up front, a MacPherson strut suspension is used while in the rear is a multi-link arrangement derived from BMW's 3-series. Steering has electrohydraulic assist. Four-wheel disc brakes with ABS are standard, the MINI Cooper and S sharing the same 10.9-inch front discs and 10.2-inch rear discs. *MINI USA*

control," DSC can use a combination of braking force and throttle control to overcome understeer or oversteer to keep a car on course.

MINI Cooper steering is by rack and pinion (2.5 turns, lock to lock) with electrohydraulic, engine-speed sensitive power assist.

Brakes

One of the most stunning reminders of how much small cars have evolved since the Mini arrived on the scene in 1959 is that the brake discs of the MINI Cooper are larger in diameter than the wheels used on the original Mini. The new car features four-wheel disc brakes consisting of 10.9-inch vented rotors up front and 10.2-inch solid rotors at the rear. Both the Cooper and Cooper S share this setup.

Another big technological advance since 1959 is the four-channel antilock braking system (ABS) that is also standard equipment on all MINI Coopers. Further enhancements that are part of the MINI Cooper brake package are electronic brakeforce distribution (EBD) and corner brake control (CBC). EBD controls the distribution of braking force between the front and rear wheels. It provides optimum braking power distribution under different load conditions, coming into effect well before ABS is required.

CBC controls brake load forces from side to side, especially if hard braking is applied during cornering. It supplies more brakeforce to the outside front wheel to counteract oversteer and also allows for more brakeforce to the rear wheels for added stopping power and stability.

Wheels and Tires

MINI Coopers come with a variety of wheel and tire combinations. A flat-tire monitor, which uses the ABS sensors to detect differences in a given wheel's revolutions per minute as compared to its opposite side counterpart, is standard equipment. The wheel and tire lineup starts on the base U.S.

A MINI Cooper fitted with the optional 16x6.5-inch five-star alloys and 195/55 R-16 tires, and the optional sport suspension plus with stiffer anti-sway bars should offer handling comparable to that of the Cooper S. It's not a bad way to go if you can live without the additional 48 horsepower that comes with the S. *MINI USA*

MINI Cooper with 5.5-inch-wide, 15-inch alloy wheels of a seven-hole design with 175/65R-15 all-season radial tires. A similar size wheel and tire combination with an eight-spoke design is also available. All-season run-flat tires, 195/55R-16, mounted on 6.5x16-inch "five-spoke star" wheels are optional on both the Cooper and Cooper S. The Cooper S comes standard with 16-inch V-spoke wheels and run-flat all-season tires. Cooper S buyers can also opt for 7.0x17-inch alloy wheels with 205/45R-17 performance run-flat tires. All wheels are available in either white or silver.

Safety and Security

Economy and space efficiency were the major factors affecting the design of the original Mini. Performance was a happy by-product. The MINI Cooper was designed to deliver on all three of those aspects plus the important modern issues

of automotive safety and security. The rigid body structure features 3,800 spot welds and is rated at 24,500 Nm/degree, which means that a torsional force of 24,500 newton meters would only cause it to twist by one degree.

In addition to the previously mentioned "active safety" measures such as flat-tire monitors, run-flat tires, ABS, EBD, CBC, and DSC, the MINI Cooper sets high standards for passive safety equipment. Front air bags are of a "smart" design that can detect the strength of an impact as well as the presence of a passenger. Air bags mounted in the side of the front seats protect the driver and passenger from thoracic injury in a side impact. Additionally, all of the air bags are linked via common crash sensors to provide optimum effectiveness in any situation.

The MINI features Advanced Head Protection System II (AHPS II), which consists of air bags concealed in the side of the roof, from the A-pillar to the C-pillar, that deploy to protect occupants' heads from side impact and objects that may penetrate along the roofline. This air bag remains deployed after activation in case of secondary or tertiary side impacts, common in vehicle-to-vehicle collisions, or in the event of a rollover.

Air bag deployment also triggers an automatic fuel-cutoff switch. Also, a battery safety terminal disconnects in case of a collision.

Opposite, top: The MINI Cooper features an extremely rigid body shell that is 50 percent stiffer than that of BMW's 3-series. Side impact door beams are part of the extremely strong passenger safety cell, with crumple zones at the front and rear to absorb the impact of an accident. *MINI USA*

Opposite, bottom: The MINI Cooper is equipped with six air bags. The front air bags use "smart" technology to sense the severity of an accident, seatbelt usage, and the presence of a passenger to determine the rate of deployment. The front seats are also equipped with side air bags. The MINI also has the AHPS II (Advanced Head Protection System) that drops down from the headliner along the side of the roof to protect occupants from head injury due to the initial impact as well as possible secondary collisions or a rollover. *MINI USA*

Below: BMW's relationship, good and bad, with Rover played a major role in the long development period undergone by the MINI, which first debuted as a concept car in 1997. The lengthy time coming to market meant ample time for testing. Cold winter testing in Scandinavia saw temperatures drop as low as –40 degrees F. *MINI USA*

The present MINI Cooper plant on the outskirts of Oxford is on the site where British automobile pioneer William Morris established a factory complex in 1927. More than 600,000 Minis were built at the old plant from 1959 to 1968. BMW acquired the plant when it bought the Rover Group in 1994. Although current production is set for around 120,000 cars annually, plant capacity could be extended to about 200,000 if needed. *MINI USA*

MINI MANUFACTURING:

Making History in an Historic Plant

MINI Coopers are manufactured on the outskirts of Oxford, one of the oldest cities in England. This city, about an hour's ride to the northeast of London, is most famous as the home of Oxford University. It also is rich in U.K. automotive history as the place where William Morris began producing motorcars almost a century ago.

Morris began his career in personal transportation when he established a bicycle repair shop in the center of Oxford in 1901. The entrepreneurial Morris quickly moved from repairing bicycles to repairing automobiles. In 1913, he set up shop in a former military academy and began assembling the first automobile to bear the Morris brand. This was a small two-seater called the Morris Oxford. Two years later, in 1915, Morris came out with the larger, four-seat Morris Cowley that used an American-made (Continental) four-cylinder engine.

These early Morris cars had two things in common with today's MINI Cooper. One was distinctive styling. The rounded, semi-streamlined shape of their radiators earned them the nickname of "Bullnose Morris." The second thing is that in building these cars, Morris set a precedent that is still practiced today in building MINI Coopers. To reduce costs, Morris set up his Oxford plant to assemble cars from components purchased from outside suppliers. The current MINI factory is on the site where Morris moved his manufacturing facilities in 1927.

In conjunction with the American Budd Corporation, Morris established the Pressed Steel Company to provide all-steel closed bodies for the chassis that were being produced at this new location. Over time, Morris Motors expanded to four plants, which were located on both sides of the Oxford Ring Road that circles the city. A "trolley" was built over the highway on which car bodies would hang from a conveyor line as they were moved from one building to another.

It was the Oxford plant, referred to as Cowley, that built the original Morris Mini-Minor from 1959 to 1968. The Austin Seven versions were built at Austin's Longbridge plant in Birmingham. In all, 602,817 Minis were built at Oxford. The 1966–67 production year was the most prolific, as 94,898 cars rolled out the doors. By comparison, 100,000 new MINI Coopers were built at the revamped Oxford facilities in its first 13 months of production.

In 1990, the four facilities at Oxford were merged into one modern manufacturing plant. Four years later, further improvements were made after BMW acquired the factory as part of its purchase of the Rover Group. With an investment of more than $400 million, including a $115 million state-of-the-art paint shop, BMW made high-tech improvements to the body manufacturing facilities and final assembly area, as well as building a logistics center and new quality control area.

The Rover 75 was built at the Oxford plant before BMW passed the Rover Group along to the Phoenix Consortium (MG Rover) and production ceased in July 2000. The entire Rover 75 manufacturing line was dismantled and moved to the Phoenix Longbridge plant over the course of eight weeks during the summer of 2000. In exchange, production equipment for the new MINI, which was originally to be produced at Longbridge, was dismantled and sent to Oxford.

MINI body panels are shipped in from a plant in Swindon, about 25 miles away, for assembly in the framing department, which is 95 percent automated. The 430,000-square-foot body assembly area is "manned" by 229 high-tech Kuka robots. Special cameras perform laser triangulation tests to monitor the quality of the bodies through a range of 117 checkpoints. *MINI USA*

The MINI assembly line had been in place at Longbridge since 1999 and a few pre-production models of the MINI had been built there during the first half of 2000.

By September of 2000, work was underway at Oxford to prepare the plant for the start of MINI production in April 2001. When the dust cleared, BMW had essentially set up a new facility to produce a new car in about seven months. In addition to money spent on the 1994 improvements, BMW invested an additional $330 million to convert the plant for MINI production.

The "New" MINI Plant

Driving up to the MINI Cooper factory, which the signs out front identify as the BMW Group Plant Oxford, there is little to tip you off to the site's historic past. The old Morris Motors/British Leyland factory buildings that were once on the opposite side of the motorway are gone, along with the overhead trolley that once carried car bodies to them. At the BMW Group plant site, the buildings that produced the car bodies for their defunct counterparts have also either been demolished, replaced, or refurbished over time to accommodate production of the Rover 75 and now the MINI Cooper.

One building, the tooling shop, still remains from the era of the original Mini. BMW has saved this building to use as a visitor's center for public tours of the MINI Cooper factory.

In a way, the "new" MINI plant is also like the "new" MINI. The outside is modern but with vestiges of the past, while the inside is very high-tech. A fully automated body plant utilizes 229 robots to ensure that the torsional rigidity designed into the new MINI Cooper on the computer screen translates to the street. Adding to the complexity of building the new MINI is that, not counting the convertible, pickup, station wagon, or any of the other 133 permutations that the old Mini underwent, there are 12 different

In order to keep production flowing smoothly, Kuka maintains an engineering office right on the factory floor. An inventory of spare parts for the robots lines the walls of the assembly area.

A base coat is applied during the eight-stage paint process for each MINI. BMW invested more than $115 million in 1997 for this state-of-the-art facility in anticipation of building the new Rover 75. The car was built at Oxford until 2000, when its assembly line was transferred to Longbridge in exchange for the MINI production equipment. *MINI USA*

47

The MINI production process is as unique as the car. Wooden "skillets" allow the workers to ride along with the car as it moves through the assembly process. Electric power tools are used exclusively, providing quieter working conditions and greater accuracy in fastening assemblies.

configurations in the current MINI range. There are right- and left-hand versions of all three models, plus their sunroof-equipped variants.

The paint shop, originally intended for the Rover 75, was finished in 1997 at a cost approaching $120 million. At the time it was under construction, it was the second biggest construction project in the U.K. Only the Millennium Dome project was larger.

Because of the number of customer-selected options, MINI final assembly is virtually done by hand. The plant is the first in Europe to feature all-electric power tools (as opposed to compressed air tools) for quiet working conditions, better worker ergonomics, and precision assembly. Special wooden "skillets" move along with each car to provide workers with a comfortable platform on which to perform their duties.

Because the MINI, like those early cars William Morris built in Oxford starting in 1913, is assembled from parts that come from a number of suppliers in the U.K. (about 40 percent) and Europe, along with engines supplied by Tritec Motors of Brazil, a just-in-time supply strategy, along with effective inventory management, is employed to maximize cost efficiency. A major factor in this equation is the Integrated Logistics Center (ILC), a 215,000-square-foot warehouse that directly feeds the assembly areas. Two tunnels connect the ILC to the production floor. Trains of parts, pulled by electric tow motors, are carried through the tunnels as needed to the various assembly stages.

The ILC has 33 aisles of five-story-high racks from which parts can be gathered and quickly loaded into the universal containers that are made up into trains to be hauled off to production.

Another aspect of the ILC is what are referred to as "late-configuration areas" for parts such as bumpers, electrical harnesses, struts and dampers, and headliners which can be set up according to the build requirements and sequence of cars in the assembly process just a few hours before they are needed. These areas are actually managed by the suppliers themselves.

All MINIs Must KISS Off

KISS (Kernfertigungs-Integrierendes Steuerungs System) is the BMW computerized information system that controls the entire manufacturing process from the body-in-white to the end of the assembly line; it also performs a series of quality checks as each MINI progresses down the line. Each MINI being built has a transponder that pinpoints its exact location in the production process. A paperless trail of information is created for every car through the use of bar coding and scanning as it moves through the various stages of production. The data attained at each stage is compared to customer specifications, build sheets, and production schedules. Information collected also measures whether a car is meeting quality standards. HMI (human-machine interface) screens provide a rundown of how far along each car is in the assembly process in regard to tracking, testing, and correcting any problems. A big benefit of using electric power tools is that they can be tied into the KISS information system so that their critical torque settings can be monitored and controlled.

The Human Factor

BMW faced a number of unique challenges in staffing for the production of the new MINI. Because there was no production for about nine months while the plant was converted from the Rover 75 assembly to that for the new MINI, it was necessary to come up with ways to retain skilled employees. A program was established to allow hours earned before the conversion to be banked toward payment during the period of inactivity. Many employees were also involved in the refurbishing and conversion of the plant. About 200 associates were sent to BMW's assembly plants in Spartanburg, South Carolina, and Regensburg, Germany, for several months to become familiar with the production techniques and quality standards that would be used at Oxford.

Original plans called for a workforce of about 2,400 employees at the Oxford MINI plant. The phenomenal response to the car's introduction in the United States on March 22,

Dr. Herbert Diess, Oxford Managing Director, poses with the 100,000th MINI produced at his plant. *MINI USA*

2002 after it had already been a hit in the U.K. since its September 2001 launch caused the factory to go to a three-shift, seven day a week, 51-week work schedule that has raised the number of employees to around 4,500.

Following a MINI Down the Line

All MINIs begin their automotive lives in the highly automated (95 percent) body-in-white area of the Oxford plant. The main body panels are shipped in from facility about 25 miles away in Swindon. Teams of Kuka robots, assisted by other robotic equipment developed internally by BMW, do almost all the work within the 430,000-square-foot body assembly area. The multi-dimensional robots are able to precisely grip, bend, and weld the MINI's body parts to assure a rigid body structure. First the front end, rear end, floor, and sides are brought together before the roof, doors, and hood are attached. The 229 robots handle 100 percent of the spot welding and more than half of the stud welding.

Cameras developed by Perceptron use a special optic to perform what is called laser triangulation to assess the quality of the body structure. They are placed at four online stations and one offline robotic station to measure 117 checkpoints.

MINI USA anticipates that 98 percent of the MINIs coming to the U.S. will have a contrasting roof. Preparing and painting of the roof created a special procedure not usually undertaken in a car with such a low selling price. *MINI USA*

Despite the time and money BMW has invested in making the Oxford plant the state of the art, there is some evidence that the plant was not originally intended to build MINIs. These are the points where pedestrian traffic must use bridges to cross over the assembly lines. More amusing evidence can be found in one of the final assembly areas in the ritual performed by the robots that install the windows. It recalls the working arrangement of C3PO and R2D2 in *Star Wars*. Space restrictions prohibited the use of two lines, one on either side of the assembly line, to feed the appropriate side window glass to the robots for installation. Instead, the windows come down on one side only, where a robot is stationed to grip a window and then "hand" it over the top of the car to its associate on the other side, who applies the adhesive and sealer to it, then waits as the first robot performs a similar task on its side of the car. They then press the left and right side glass in place at the same time.

Another indication of how BMW has worked around the constraints imposed by the plant conversion is seen at points where a giant robotic claw drops down from a hole in the ceiling to spirit body assemblies to another location. Completed bodies are shuttled off from the body-in-white area to the paint shop in this manner.

Another worker-friendly timesaver is a rotisserie that rotates the car body so that a worker does not need to crawl or stoop under a car.

Unlike in the body-in-white area, the fitting of the interior pieces to the MINI is done almost entirely by hand.

Just-in-time processes are an important aspect of the Oxford assembly process. For example, the entire dash panel, including the steering wheel, steering column, instruments, switches, heating system, and wiring harness is installed as a unit, after having arrived from the manufacturing plant in Redditch, about 60 miles away. Various assemblies and parts arrive on a strict schedule to coincide with a particular vehicle on the line. Delivery trucks stay in radio contact with the plant in order to avoid delays and take alternate routes as traffic conditions dictate.

Left: Engines arrive assembled from Brazil and are mated to the transmission and front suspension/drive cradle by workers. **Above:** The entire engine/suspension assembly is then mated to the almost fully assembled car body. *MINI USA*

The 10-hour, eight-stage paint process for each MINI begins with the "pre-treatment." The car body is dipped into a wash tank to remove any debris from the assembly process, then dipped into another tank where it is coated with zinc phosphate for corrosion resistance. Next the car is ready for the application of electropaint, another important step in corrosion-proofing of the car. The process involves dipping it in a vat of paint which is electrically charged by applying 300 volts and 800 amps. This electrical charge causes the paint to adhere to both the inside and outside of the body structure. Baking the body in an oven then cures the paint. This process has both efficiency and environmental benefits. Because of the way the MINI body structure has been designed, more than 90 percent of the paint goes onto the car during this process while what remains is cleaned and used again.

Next comes the application of seam sealer, underbody coating, and sound deadening. The seam sealer is applied to all critical seams

MINIs arrive by crane from the engine assembly area and, after the wheels are installed, hit the floor as a fully assembled automobile. At that point a bit of fuel is added to the tank and the car goes through a brief running check.

both manually and by robots. Robots apply a coating to the underside of the body, which primarily serves to protect it from stone chips and other road damage. A secondary function of this coating is that it also acts as a sound deadener. Thick padding, for sound insula-

tion, is applied to various points inside of the car body.

Surfacer paint is then applied to all the areas that will be visible in the completed car. It is applied robotically to the exterior and manually to the interior. Besides enhancing the final color

After a quick systems test, the completed MINI is ready to be handed over for delivery to market.

coat, the polyester-based surfacer paint smoothes out the rough surfaces from the electropaint process and, because of its high solids content, improves the overall paint job's resistance to chipping.

Before the final color coat is applied, the car is lightly sanded. Sanding dust is removed by a spraying of compressed air and wiping with a tack cloth. Final cleaning is by a unique "feather duster" machine, similar to an automatic car wash machine but with feathers instead of brushes. The final color coat is a water-based paint that is applied both manually and by automatic spray machines. The car body is then baked in an infrared oven.

Cars coming off the line are randomly checked to assure that quality standards are being met.

The contrasting roof paint is applied robotically after the final color coat. Following that is the clear coat and another heat treatment.

The final step is more corrosion-proofing through the application of cavity wax to all of the car's hollow sections where water is prone to collect. The body shell is heated and then rocked back and forth to ensure that the wax penetrates into all the critical areas.

Total time for painting and corrosion-proofing of the body shell is 10 hours. Cars are painted in production line sequence according to customer orders and not in batches according to color.

The first step of final assembly actually involves some disassembly, as the doors are taken off the painted body and whisked off to another line where they are fitted with windows and interior trim before meeting up with their respective body farther down the main line.

The body is placed on an individual wooden work platform called a "skillet," which provides workers with a wide work area that moves with the car through the assembly operations. The height of the car body on the assembly line changes according to the process being performed to give workers optimum ergonomic working conditions. A rotisserie arrangement allows the car to swivel 90 degrees so that wiring and other work underneath the car can be done at a comfortable and convenient angle. Various power tools are used to grip and move heavier parts into place. One of the more interesting of these devices is a hovercraft-style jack that floats along the floor to move and then hold the rear exhaust system in place while a worker attaches the bolts.

The MINI's four-cylinder Tritec-built engines arrive fully assembled from Brazil. They are mated to the clutch and gearbox in the powertrain sub-assembly area. The front suspension also comes together in this area. The engine/gearbox assembly then joins the front suspension and they are mounted to the car body. The rear suspension is also assembled before being attached as a unit to the car body.

The wheels and tires are the last parts fitted before the Mini can roll off the line.

Finally, each MINI must pass a thorough battery of tests and a short test drive before it is turned over for delivery.

An early media event to announce the arrival of the MINI to the U.S. had stunt driver Russ Swift emulating the Minis featured in the film *The Italian Job. MINI USA*

the faddish fate of vehicles like the PT Cruiser, which saw its popularity nosedive as soon as dealers' inventories were increased. The objective was to avoid making the MINI a fad, and to give it a longer-lasting presence by creating a cult of MINI owners and customers. To do so involved unorthodox, guerrilla-style marketing techniques that appealed to select customers looking for a unique vehicle.

Reintroducing the MINI to America

Thirty-five years had elapsed since the last new Mini was officially imported for sale in the United States, so the launch of the MINI brand in America came closer to being an introduction than a reintroduction. This situation was not lost on some people within BMW management, who initially felt that Americans, in the middle of a torrid love affair with trucks and SUVs, would be reluctant to embrace such a small car. With only about 10,000 original Minis being sold from 1960 through 1967, it seemed that the MINI could not even count on tradition as a sales tool.

"After 35 years, Mini awareness was negligible," reports Jack Pitney, MINI USA General Manager. "Less than 2 percent of Americans knew what a Mini was. There were a lot of people [at BMW] wondering whether MINI should come back to the U.S."

Many different scenarios were played out over the years by BMW management regarding the MINI's future in America. Fortunately, a small but rabid band of Mini enthusiasts within the BMW organization worked to sell the idea that the MINI could be a hit in America. One of those people was Pitney, at the time the communications manager for BMW North America.

During his college days, Pitney had owned a 1969 MGB, a 1970 MGB-GT, and a Triumph TR-7, a car that even the self-professed anglophile auto fanatic describes as a "total disaster." He admits that Minis were a bit of a mystery to him until BMW acquired the Rover Group. Soon after, he asked to go to England to become better acquainted with the Mini.

"The people in Germany [at BMW headquarters] were so excited that somebody in America cared enough to ask, that they put together a weeklong immersion course in Mini," he recalls. "It was fabulous; I got to drive the very first Mini that came off the line on August 26, 1959, and then a current 'classic' Mini, red with white bonnet stripes and a Union Jack on the roof. I went away with a great appreciation for the brand."

When the decision was made to start a small team to market the MINI brand in the United States, Tom Purves, vice president of BMW North America, offered Pitney the job.

Pitney backed up his enthusiasm and optimism regarding the MINI's viability in America

Jack Pitney, the 38–year-old selected to lead the introduction of the MINI to America, has been with BMW since 1995. He was formerly head of corporate communications for BMW North America. His prior experience includes working at GCI Group in Los Angeles, where he oversaw the launch of the Infiniti luxury car division of Nissan. *MINI USA*

LET'S PUT AWAY THE MIDDLE FINGER.
Let's lay off the horn.
Let's volunteer jumper cables.
Let's pay a stranger's toll.
Let's be considerate of cyclists.
And for crying out loud, let's all remember to turn off those blinkers. **LET'S MOTOR.**™

This print ad is an excerpt from *The Book of Motoring*, **which itself was bound into auto enthusiasts' publications.** *MINI USA*

with solid business reasoning. "The important thing is that we don't aspire to sell 100,000 cars (in the U.S.). We're doing 20,000 cars, a relatively modest number in a market of 17 million vehicles."

Pitney started with four or five MINI loyalists and soon expanded to a team of 30 employees whose jobs are 100 percent dedicated to the MINI brand. Pitney has 11 people working directly for him at the New Jersey headquarters with seven more in field offices around the country. The rest work within other departments of BMW North America, such as the warranty department, dedicated to handling MINI-related tasks.

Pitney is quick to point out that the other 1,120 other employees at BMWNA also perform some services for MINI. It is part of the unique MINI business management plan for the U.S. that there is a separate organization to ensure the necessary brand identity while at the same time, for reasons of profitability and efficiency regarding the relatively small sales volume, making use of the larger overall corporate infrastructure whenever possible.

This idea carries over to the dealership level, where it was important for brand identity to create a separate showroom and sales staff, yet it was more efficient and profitable to share the parts and service areas of an existing BMW sales facility.

Launching the MINI Brand

"This is not the 'new' Mini launch," Jack Pitney told members of the press assembled for a preview drive of the MINI Cooper in March 2002. "This is the MINI launch."

What Pitney was telling everyone was that the MINI is being sold not as a new car but as a new brand, one that is creating a new segment in the American marketplace. BMW considers the MINI a "premium" small car.

"Small cars have historically been inexpensive, let's call them cheap, boxes of transportation to get you from point A to point B. This car has all the build quality of a BMW, unbelievable technology, and it's a hoot to drive," Pitney explained. "It is really going to change people's perceptions about what is possible with a small car."

By the same token, Pitney makes the point that the MINI is not a mass-market car. It is not meant to sell in large numbers because it is "not for everybody."

"What we really want to do is build MINI into an icon like it is in England, Europe, and Asia," Pitney declared.

He cites Apple computers and Harley-Davidson motorcycles as products that have achieved icon status. The importance of achieving icon status is that it means a product is more than a fad or trend. Icons also transcend class boundaries, something equally important to a vehicle being sold as a premium small car. The original Mini with its list of royal and celebrity owners serves as the perfect example of this trait.

Who Is a MINI Customer?

One of the first things that the MINI marketing team discovered is that their clientele is different from people shopping for BMWs. The price of the MINI appeals to a younger buyer more than the typical BMW customer. But Pitney feels that there is more to the MINI's appeal than a low price.

"I think at its heart and soul, MINI is about excitement," he says. "Everything about the brand, including the people who are drawn to it, is very extroverted. They are early adopters, people who are into having fun, and love a very connected driving experience. They want to be first with the latest and the greatest."

Pitney feels the above characteristics cannot be confined to one age group. He cites the example of a San Francisco bay area dealer who in one day

Research showed that potential MINI buyers preferred to discover products on their own rather than relying on advertising claims. MINI USA aided in the discovery process by driving an SUV around select cities with a MINI mounted on the roof rack. *MINI USA*

WHAT ARE YOU DOING FOR FUN THIS WEEKEND?

had customers wanting to get on the waiting list for a new MINI that ranged in age from a 15-year-old boy planning ahead for his 16th birthday and his new driver's license to a 72-year-old grandmother eager to get into a Cooper S.

So who, then, is the typical customer according to the research conducted by the MINI team?

"We kept trying to find a demographic because it makes our job easier, but the only thing we found is that there is none," Pitney responds. "Demographics are irrelevant when it comes to owning a MINI. It's a mindset. The type of person you are is what makes you a MINI person."

What Pitney calls the "MINI mindset" is not determined by chronological age or gender but by an attitude that enjoys individuality. The new MINI, like the original Mini, does not fit into a traditional automotive category. This uniqueness appeals to individuals who prefer to stand apart

Rather than parade MINIs around the field during halftime or between innings, Pitney's marketing team had the cars sit in the stands. A MINI attended two crucial baseball games between the Oakland A's and Seattle Mariners. This one was ready for some *Monday Night Football* exposure. *MINI USA*

MINI Ride is not set up to accept money, but judging by the long waiting period most customers are experiencing, it may be worth spending a quarter or two every day for a short spin until your real MINI is delivered. *MINI USA*

from the crowd. It also creates an emotional bond between the vehicle and its owner that is reflected in the loyalty and devotion that owners have expressed toward the original Mini over the years.

Guerrilla Marketing Tactics

Not having a "typical customer" meant that the MINI could not rely on a typical marketing program. In fact, one thing that the market research carried out by the MINI team did show about prospective MINI buyers is that they hate being marketed to. Because of this, the MINI team relies on what are referred to as guerrilla marketing tactics to create public awareness.

"They [MINI customers] would rather discover something and be the first to share it with their friends," according to Pitney. "So we try to come up with ways for them to 'discover' MINI."

One of the more extreme guerrilla marketing tactics used by the MINI team to let people 'discover' the MINI was to mount a MINI on the roof rack of a behemoth Ford Excursion and drive it around a city with a sign that asked "What are you doing for fun this weekend?" The idea was that driving an enormous SUV was work and the MINI was meant to be fun and a way to escape the humdrum. Business cards were handed out to those whose curiosity was piqued by the MINI's piggyback rides. The cards featured a picture of a MINI on one side and "Coming to America – www.miniusa.com" on the other. People could then go to the website and "discover" the story behind the MINI for themselves.

The MINI was also exposed to the public at traditional marketing venues such as shopping malls and sporting events, but with a zany twist to appeal to those who appreciated the Mini mindset.

"Anybody can put a car on the field and drive it around," said Pitney.

What the MINI team did was to arrange for a MINI to have front row "seating" at a couple of Oakland A's baseball games. The tongue-in-cheek press release following the MINI's appearance stated that although the MINI is historically better known for its love of motorsports, "we know that the MINI enjoys a fun occasion."

The MINI also appeared at a shopping mall in Santa Ana, California. Not as the run-of-the-mill new car display but as a whimsical "coin operated" MINI-ride with a sign above the coin slot that read, "Insert $16,850 in quarters only." As a precaution, the MINI people put up an "out of order" sign just in case someone decided to crack open a MINI-sized piggy bank and call their bluff.

Guerrilla marketing tactics created a big impression but cost less than expensive television and print advertising campaigns. Just as guerilla fighters employ methods to create the impression that they are everywhere, guerrilla marketing has a similar effect.

MINI did not run a print ad until March 2002. As MINIs arrived in dealerships for the sales kickoff date of March 22, an advertising campaign using print ads and outdoor advertising was announced. The campaign, with a budget estimated at $35 million, was unusual in that it did not include television or radio spots but concentrated on car buffs and certain lifestyle magazines, plus billboards in key markets including Times Square.

MINI Works the World Wide Web

The Internet has played a major role in the MINI marketing scheme. MINI fans around the world got their first live look at the production version of the new MINI Cooper at the same time as the international motoring press via a webcast on September 28, 2000, from Paris at the Mondial de l'Automobile 2000 auto show.

The MINI's web presence goes many layers deep. From the main site of MINI.com, individuals can click on the flag of their home country and be directed to a website tailored to provide specific information pertaining to MINI Coopers in their homeland. For curiosity's sake, they can click another country's flag to discover what is going on in relation to the MINI in other parts of the world.

In January 2002, the miniusa.com website was beefed up with enhanced graphics and an enlarged database of information in anticipation of the March 22 kickoff date for MINI sales in the United States. To appeal to the tech-savvy nature of MINI enthusiasts, state-of-the-art programs such as Macromedia Flash 4.0 and virtual 3-D viewers are intrinsic elements of the website that keep interest levels high by providing informative and entertaining diversions, including hidden messages and other surprises along with detours that lead to other parts of the website.

A "Build Your Own Mini" section provides comprehensive product and pricing information so that prospective MINI customers will be well prepared when it comes time to visit the actual, instead of virtual, showroom. Prospective MINI owners can also check out available financing and special lease plans to get a clearer idea of how much MINI they can afford per month before they hit the "brick-and-mortar" dealership.

The website also helps customers locate their nearest MINI dealer. Once a nearby dealership is determined, customers can then click on a link at miniusa.com to obtain specific information regarding directions and business hours.

Besides shopping for a MINI itself, the website has a section where MINI fans can shop for MINI MotoringGear. This is merchandise ranging from clothing to cuckoo clocks, all uniquely styled to appeal to the MINI enthusiast and available for purchase through the website as well as at dealers.

Movies are an integral part of the MINI website landscape. They usually depict lighthearted episodes of MINI motoring. One of the first movie clips delivered the message that the MINI was now available in America. A MINI driver is shown driving through the desert, grooving to the radio, and generally enjoying his drive in a MINI. Suddenly a police car appears and pulls him over. The policeman, who turns out to be an English bobby, leans in and informs the MINI driver that he has been stopped for driving on the wrong side of the road. "This is America," exclaims the driver. The bobby appears stunned for a second, eyes the arid scenery, and then recovers with typical British aplomb by answering back "Right then. Carry on."

According to Jack Pitney, the motivating force behind the website is to build up an ongoing relationship with MINI owners and enthusiasts.

"We want to keep people in the loop as to whatever we are doing," he says.

In fact, under the heading "Get In The Loop" MINI fans can register their e-mail address to receive the latest MINI announcements and press releases.

MINI owners can register at the "Owners' Lounge" area which provides an online database for monitoring maintenance and service information about their car, along with warranty updates and other pertinent information. It is also possible to review the status of any MINI loan or lease financed through BMW in the Owners' Lounge area.

MINI buyers can actually track the progress of their car through the manufacturing and delivery process. For example, they can find out if it is in the paint shop at the Oxford plant, waiting at the shipping port, crossing "the pond" aboard ship, or on terra firma in the U.S.

"We knew that people will have to wait two, three, four, even six months for a car so we created the 'Make Waiting Fun' program," said Pitney. "Once you have a firm order in and we know who you are, we'll send you an e-mail, get into an electronic conversation with you, and we'll send you all kinds of things."

As the delivery date approaches, the buyer will be informed by an e-mail that "your MINI likes the same music that you do." The waiting owner will be asked for a list of favorite radio stations so that when he or she picks up their car, this personalized set of radio stations will have been preset on the radio buttons. MINI has also partnered with Rhino Records to put together compilation CDs of different types of music so that an owner can choose one that best fits their interest. It will be in the CD player when the car is delivered.

Last but not least in the Make Waiting Fun program is the Unauthorized Owner's Manual that Pitney says, "tells you all the cool things you discover about your car after you've lived with it for a while, only we send it to you ahead of time." This book contains gems like the best place to hide the keys if you are going for a jog, where to stash CDs, and the fact that the MINI's headlights remain lit if you open the bonnet. This last bit of information comes with suggestions for using this feature to search for a lost kitty in a tree or add a spotlight effect to your next outdoor party.

Let's Motor

The philosophy of "Motoring" is a theme that runs through the marketing of the MINI in the United States. Jack Pitney explained that "motoring" is a concept that combines the MINI's heritage, personality, and technical attributes.

"Motoring is a British term," said Pitney. "In America, everyone, even BMW, talks about being the best driver's car. The ads say 'Driver's Wanted,' or 'the Ultimate Driving Machine,' even just plain 'Driven.' We don't want to fight on that battleground because the MINI is not about going from point A to B; it is more about going from A to Z and all the points in between. Motoring captures that message."

Pitney summed up this stance when he said, "We have a unique opportunity to define the next phase in the history of an automotive icon. As the new MINI is a distinctive car without parallel in the U.S. market, we have chosen Motoring as our unique brand positioning. The theme of Motoring will run through every aspect of our business."

Cutting through the smoke of all the marketing-speak, what exactly does Motoring mean? An early press release, dated August 2001, from the MINI people offers the following explanation. They call it an "enlightened form of driving." The MINI is all about exploration, discovery, and exhilaration. Motoring is not concerned with gender, age, or social status. Motoring is meant to represent the MINI's spirit of action and adventure. The MINI people claim, "Driving is a term about cars and the road. Motoring is a unifying religion, a new, more enlightened form of driving

"Let's Motor" doubles as both the MINI mantra and its advertising catch phrase. Pitney explains that while other car companies stress an aggressive approach to driving, the MINI extols a more relaxed attitude of motoring. Driving a MINI on Lombard Street in San Francisco as opposed to a twisting mountain road is more in the benign spirit of motoring. *MINI USA*

67

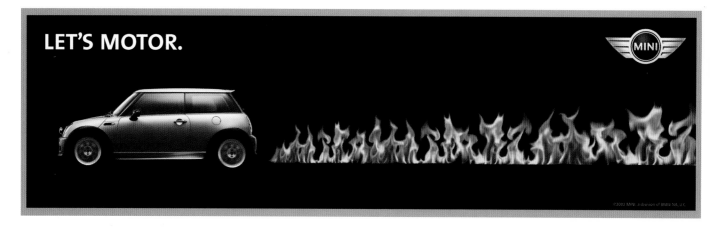

The guerrilla marketing approach favored by Pitney uses unusual methods such as billboard advertising. This ad also appeared as the first MINI print ad. It did not run until March 2002 and only because Pitney wanted to protect the phrase "Let's Motor." *MINI USA*

that takes advice from the back seat and lets people in our lanes. When one drives a MINI, one's outlook on life changes. And so the world becomes a better place."

Cynics may feel that the last statement reads more like the automotive philosophy of (Grateful) Dead-head Volvo drivers. Market research studies conducted by MINI at major metropolitan markets in the U.S. revealed, however, that the prospective MINI customers understood and appreciated Motoring as a word and as a theme. They saw the term "Let's Motor" as an invitation that expresses a "let's get going" mentality.

The MINI team believes in motoring. Only time will tell if it sustains a lasting buzz for the MINI or simply becomes another buzzword.

Dealership Network

BMW North America claims 341 automobile, 321 sports activity vehicle, and 153 motorcycle retailers in the United States. The MINI, however,

MINI advertising tends to be cute and unusual, but it still manages to get its message delivered. *MINI USA*

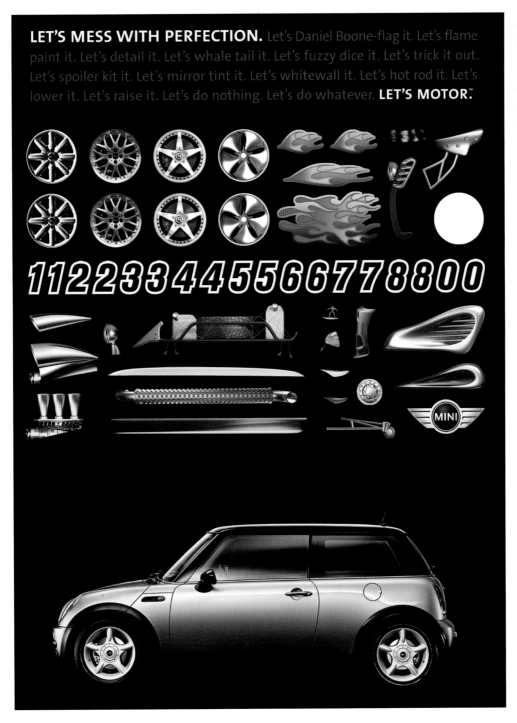

LET'S MESS WITH PERFECTION. Let's Daniel Boone-flag it. Let's flame paint it. Let's detail it. Let's whale tail it. Let's fuzzy dice it. Let's trick it out. Let's spoiler kit it. Let's mirror tint it. Let's whitewall it. Let's hot rod it. Let's lower it. Let's raise it. Let's do nothing. Let's do whatever. **LET'S MOTOR.**

Another surprise bound into auto magazines was a sheet of stickers with which you could customize your MINI. At Halloween, the miniusa.com website offered a full-size, 120-page, downloadable MINI costume for people who wanted to dress up their non-MINI for trick or treating. *MINI USA*

Pitney and his team hold brainstorming sessions regarding various marketing ideas and items, but even he was amazed that well before the MINI went on sale on March 22, 2002, more than 3,000 MINI cuckoo clocks, priced at $85, had been sold. *MINI USA*

require, in some cases, an investment as high as $350,000, an overwhelming number of prospective dealers flooded MINI USA with proposals seeking a MINI dealership agreement.

Pitney wanted dealers who were willing to rethink the way they sold cars. A major step was to hire people who had never worked in the auto industry but were used to working in companies that demanded a high level of customer service.

"We've hired a lot of people from Nordstrom and Starbucks," said Pitney. Besides selling vehicles, MINI dealers are also expected to properly showcase and sell the line of MINI MotoringGear.

"Our commitment to the dealers is that we are not just introducing MINI Cooper and MINI Cooper S," declared Pitney. "We're introducing the MINI Cooper brand, a brand that ultimately has to have its own self-grown product. There are so many different directions that we can take this brand."

After the first two months of business, with sales totaling 4,142 cars through May 31, 2002, Pitney and his dealers had every reason to be optimistic. The original first-year U.S. sales estimate of 20,000 units was bumped up to 25,000 as production was increased at Oxford to meet the increased demand.

Merchandising the MINI

Jack Pitney may have felt confident about selling 20,000 MINIs in the U.S., but no one could have predicted that thousands of MINI cuckoo clocks would have been sold before a single car was delivered. The $85 clocks, which resemble a MINI speedometer with a pod from which a MINI pops out on the hour, were sold through the miniusa.com website during the first three months of 2002.

An *Automotive News* story reported that dealers who sell MINIs at list price have a profit margin of 10 percent, making sales of MINI merchandise and accessories an important source

is sold through a separate retail network of 70 dealerships in select areas of the country. At the official launch date of March 22, 2002, almost 60 of these dealers were open and ready for business, with the remaining coming on line thereafter.

The dealerships are located in 29 states within major metropolitan and progressive urban areas, selected because they were where market research indicated MINI customers were most likely to live. Standards to qualify included a commitment to add separate (from the BMW side) facilities, and a sales and technical staff dedicated to the MINI brand. Despite the fact that meeting these standards could

Another popular item is the remote-control scale model MINI. MINI MotoringGear items are sold over the website and at dealerships. Pitney feels that MINI dealers can be like Harley-Davidson dealers, where lifestyle items are more profitable than the vehicles being sold. *MINI USA*

for increasing a dealer's bottom line. Pitney agrees with them.

"This is a big opportunity," he said when asked about catering to the MINI aftermarket. "We don't see any car company doing a particularly good job at this. The best Harley-Davidson dealers make more on lifestyle and accessory products than on the motorcycles themselves."

No one understands this better than Kerri Martin, MINI marketing manager, who worked for Harley-Davidson before joining BMW. To get a fresh approach on the marketing of MINI

A T-shirt emblazoned with the MINI speedometer is one of the more mainstream apparel items aimed at MINI fanatics. Renat Aruh, MINI accessories manager, was hired from the fashion industry to create a line of products that are more than just promotional items but have a close relationship with the MINI brand. On another shirt, Aruh had designers incorporate an elbow patch made from the same material as the MINI's seat covering. *MINI USA*

MotoringGear, Renat Aruh, the MINI accessories manager, was hired from the fashion industry. Aruh feels that MINI accessories and clothing have to be more than promotional items. They have to be part of the MINI lifestyle. Therefore, the items offered were custom-designed in order to relate to the MINI brand.

Aruh would like MINI enthusiasts to see the dealership as a retail center where they can stop by periodically to look for new merchandise. She thinks that having mirrors and even dressing rooms in the dealership is a good idea.

Besides a designer clothing line of jackets, shirts, and hats, MINI accessories include items

Co-branding may not be part of motoring, but it is part of the MINI marketing plan. The first of what Renat Aruh refers to as "synergistic relationships" with premium products is a set of MINI Travel Gear luggage by Samsonite. *MINI USA*

traditionally sold by automakers including a watch, driving gloves, pens, key chains, umbrellas, coffee cups, CD cases, model cars, and a MINI "baby racer" with trailer for MINI drivers in training. All have a unique MINI style to them.

MINI is also co-branding accessories. Fall of 2002 will see the debut of MINI Travel Gear, a joint development between MINI and Samsonite.

MINI handling is excellent even when compared to a rear-drive car. There does not seem to be much difference between the 15-inch and 16-inch wheels other than slightly better ride quality on the smaller wheels and tires. *MINI USA*

Chapter Six

DRIVING THE MINI:
New Versus Old

When asked to compare driving the original Mini to a new MINI, the man who piloted the Mini Cooper to its most significant racing victory—the 1964 Monte Carlo Rally—just laughed.

"The old one smelled of petrol and had a lot of water leaks," says Paddy Hopkirk, who many consider the quintessential Mini driver. "This new one doesn't."

The jaunty Irishman used humor so as not to dampen the warm memories many people have for the old car, but brushing 40-plus years of nostalgia aside, there is no comparison between the two cars. The old Mini is too small, inside and out, underpowered, and uncomfortable to make sense as a daily driver by today's standards. There are also the usual reliability and maintenance issues that are just as much iconic symbols of old British cars as is the Mini itself. The Mini may have been ahead of its time, but four decades of high-tech automotive engineering have overtaken even the brilliant foresight that Alec Issigonis had in designing his small wonder car.

Fortunately, the new MINI captures the personality and flair of the old car and combines them with the performance, comfort, and safety expected from a twenty-first century car to provide similar driving thrills.

Cooper versus Cooper S

It is easy to fall into the trap of "more is better" when comparing the standard Cooper version of the MINI to the supercharged Cooper S. The S comes equipped with more horsepower (163 bhp versus 115 bhp), more gears (a six-speed versus a five-speed manual transmission), larger 16-inch wheels and tires, thicker anti-sway bars, and stiffer springs. There is no arguing that the S is the speedier of the two models going from 0 to 60 mph in, according to BMW's figures, 6.9 seconds while the Cooper is about a second and a half slower, needing 8.5 seconds to do so. Top speed of the Cooper S is also 11 miles per hour faster, 135 mph versus 124 mph.

Remember, however, that one of the original Mini's charms and attributes was its ability to perform better than its numbers would indicate. The same holds true when comparing the

Paddy Hopkirk won the Monte Carlo Rally in 1964 to put himself and the Mini in the motorsports spotlight during the sixties. Hopkirk can do as many miraculous things with a new MINI as he did with the old one. His Irish wit matches his driving skills, but most of his stories are better left out of print.

Cooper to the Cooper S. The Cooper S is a stunning performer given its engine size and cost, but its Cooper sibling provides real-world performance that is also quite remarkable, especially when its price tag, about $3,000 less than the S, is factored into the equation. The original Mini was never a threat at the drag strip but judicious use of the power available made it an exciting car to drive and one that could hold its own in traffic. The same is true of the standard Cooper. Those too lazy or unskilled to properly work the gearbox to maintain engine revolutions in the car's power band will be disappointed in the car's performance. In truth, those same people would probably consider the original Mini to be a bit of a slug.

Unfortunately, both the Cooper S and Cooper share one negative aspect in engine performance. The 1.6-liter Pentagon engine has very little power to offer below 2,500 rpm. Both the Cooper S and Cooper stutter off the line unless a healthy dose of engine revs accompanies the clutch release. This lack of low-end torque is also what makes it important to keep stirring the gears in a base Cooper, especially when traveling on a twisty road. Downshifting is helpful when approaching a corner to maintain engine revs above 3,000 rpm, or the car will bog down through the corner until the engine works back up to its power band. This is where the closer-ratio six-speed of the Cooper S offers an advantage. Either way, both gearboxes are exceptionally smooth to operate and belie the fact that they are part of a front-wheel drive system.

In terms of braking and handling, both cars share the same brake system and the Cooper can be fitted with the sportier suspension and 16-inch tire/wheel combination of the Cooper S. Given that the Cooper weighs in about 200 pounds lighter than the S, adding the sportier tires and suspension should result in a slight performance edge as far as stopping and cornering. The Cooper S does have the exclusive advantage of the optional 17-inch wheels and performance tires. On the other hand, the non-run-flat 15-inch wheels offered on the standard Cooper seem to provide the most comfortable ride. Either car thrives on sinuous two-lane roads. Handling is excellent and comparable to the best rear-drive sports cars. There is very little front-drive understeer. Paddy Hopkirk claimed that the new MINI was even better for performing "handbrake turns" than his old rally cars.

The bottomline is that BMW has built a pretty solid, well-balanced foundation for the new MINI. Boy racers and hardcore performance drivers will have to have a Cooper S, but most people should be able to configure a standard Cooper that will be fun to drive and provide the anticipated "Mini" driving experience while staying well south of $20,000.

Just sitting inside either version of the MINI Cooper is almost as much fun as driving it. The large round speedometer mounted in the middle of the dash may recall Minis of the past, but it

The MINI tachometer sits directly in front of the driver on top of the steering column. *MINI USA*

The center stack below the speedometer houses the stereo, air conditioning, and toggle switches for windows, door locks, auxiliary lights, and optional DSC traction control. The design is a blend of high-tech and an old-school look, but the buttons and switches are tiny and bunched together. *MINI USA*

This is a Cooper S with the optional navigation system. The nav display takes over the central speedometer spot. On cars so equipped, the speedometer moves next to the tachometer, perched on top of the steering column. *MINI USA*

sacrifices function for form. Considering the style points it garners, this is not a bad trade-off unless one is traveling through a school zone or radar trap where it is essential to precisely monitor one's speed. The good news is that the tachometer could not be in a better spot, perched atop the steering column and easily visible through the two-spoke steering wheel. Sporting drivers will quickly learn to calculate speed versus engine revs to further relegate the speedometer to its use solely as a styling cue. Another solution would be to order the optional navigation system, which then moves into the large circular center space vacated by the speedometer as it joins the tachometer in twin nacelles on the steering column.

Standard on either MINI Cooper is an AM/FM/CD stereo mounted in a center console

SPECIFICATIONS: 2002 MINI COOPER AND COOPER S

	MINI Cooper	MINI Cooper S
Transmission	five-speed manual (R65)	six-speed manual (Getrag 285)
Gear ratios (:1)		
1/2/3	3.42/1.95/1.33/	11.41/7.18/5.40
4/5/6	1.04/.85/na	4.41/3.66/2.97
Length	142.8 inches	143.9 inches
Width	66.5 inches	66.5 inches
Height	55.4 inches	55.8 inches
Wheelbase	97.1 inches	97.1 inches
Turning Circle	35 feet	35 feet
Overhang:		
Front	24.5 inches	25.5 inches
Rear	21.1 inches	21.3 inches
Track:		
Front	57.4 inches	57.2 inches
Rear	57.7 inches	57.5 inches
Fuel Tank capacity	13.2 gallons	13.2 gallons
Unladen weight	2,315 pounds	2,513 pounds
Engine	1.6-liter four-cylinder	1.6-liter four-cylinder w/super charger and air/air intercooler
Horsepower	115 at 6,000 rpm	163 at 6,000 rpm
Torque	110 at 4,500 rpm	155 at 4,000 rpm
Compression ratio	10.6:1	8.3:1
Drag coefficient Cd	0.35	0.36
Top speed:	124 mph	135 mph
0–60 mph	8.5 seconds	6.9 seconds
Brakes:		
Front	10.9-inch vented disc	10.9-inch vented disc
Rear	10.2-inch disc	10.2-inch disc
Wheels	5.5x15-inch alloy	6.5x16-inch alloy
Tires	175/65 R-15 all-season	195/55 R-16 all-season run-flat

along with the heating, ventilation, and air conditioning controls. An optional Harman Kardon audio system includes eight speakers along with goodies like vehicle speed-sensitive equalization and a special driver-only acoustic setting. Automatic air conditioning is another worthwhile option. Mounted below the stereo and HVAC controls is a row of toggle switches that work the power windows, fog lights, and central locking system, plus a deactivation switch for the

continued on page 82

MINI COOPER ALTERNATIVES

Because the MINI Cooper is really in a segment—if not a class—of its own, it really has no direct competitors in the marketplace. There are a few vehicles that can be considered alternatives. The first two that come to mind are the VW Beetle and the PT Cruiser. The Beetle, of course, preceded the MINI Cooper as a modern version of another innovative car built for the masses. The difference is that the new Beetle merely employs retro exterior styling that resembles the original on a

Sharing a lot in common with the MINI, including a powerful S model (180 horsepower Turbo) is the Volkswagen Beetle. The MINI Cooper handles better and better utilizes interior space.

chassis that is borrowed from a modern Volkswagen, the Golf. The old Beetle had a flat, air-cooled engine in the rear and rear-wheel drive. The new Beetle has a liquid-cooled engine mounted up front that drives the front wheels. The characteristics that made people buy an original Beetle instead of a Mini, and vice versa, probably will apply to the buyers of the new cars as well.

The PT Cruiser has the retro look but no real original forefather. Not really offering much in the way of sporty handling or driving thrills, the PT Cruiser gets by on offering the space and utility of a minivan hidden under the exterior trappings of a street rod at a price range very close to the MINI Cooper. A turbocharged version for the 2003 model year should liven up the PT Cruiser's performance level.

The Audi TT has unique styling that, like the MINI, is modern with hints of nostalgia. All-wheel drive and turbocharged (225 hp) performance, however, come at a price that is almost double that of the Cooper S.

The 170-horsepower Ford SVT Focus is a worthy competitor to the Cooper S in terms of performance and handling, with a price closer to the base model. It loses out with edgy styling that appeals to the video game rally crowd.

The Audi TT has a unique retro look and offers sporty performance and handling in both front-wheel and all-wheel drive. The TT lacks the interior capacity of the MINI Cooper and is much more expensive, with the base coupe priced almost $12,000 more than a standard MINI Cooper.

The Ford Focus SVT and Honda Civic Si compare favorably to the Cooper S in performance and price, but their edgy styling appeals to a smaller audience than the Cooper S. These cars also have limited interior space.

After looking at the alternatives, the new MINI, like its predecessor, makes its mark by offering a package unlike any other vehicle.

Another car that falls short of the MINI in the styling department is the 160-horsepower Honda Civic Si. It drives European, but looks Japanese.

continued from page 79

optional DSC. The console's overall appearance is retro chic but the various switches and controls are small and closely bunched, requiring some time for familiarization.

The six-way adjustable manual seats that are standard on the MINI Cooper are reasonably comfortable, but the optional (standard on Cooper S) sports seats are preferable in terms of comfort and appearance. No power seats are available on either model. The rear seats fold forward individually for increased rear cargo space. The trunk is not very deep (with the seats in the upright position) but makes up for this in width and height. BMW says a 36-inch television will easily fit in the back of a MINI.

The MINI Cooper's interior is spacious even compared with cars that are much larger on the outside. Passengers well over six feet tall can ride comfortably for short distances in the rear seats. Up front there is plenty of elbow, leg, and headroom for people up to six-foot-seven. MINI USA Product Manager Kevin Philips, who measures six-foot-four, loves to demonstrate the interior room by sitting in the front seat, then climbing into the back seat directly behind it and still having a comfortable amount of legroom.

The optional dual-pane sunroof covers 60 percent of the MINI Cooper roof to provide a panoramic overhead view. The best part is that adding the sunroof does not encroach on any of the MINI's ample headroom. Speaking of the roof, MINI USA expects that 98 percent of the MINIs coming to America will have the contrasting black or white roof paint scheme. Buyers will also have a choice of optional roof graphics that include a checkerboard, U.S. flag, or the Union Jack.

Six-way adjustable leather-covered sport seats are standard on the Cooper S. They are comfortable and well bolstered for spirited driving. *MINI USA*

Opposite, top: An alloy patina finish is part of the Cooper S interior treatment. *MINI USA*

Opposite, bottom: The standard seats and interior of the MINI Cooper are not as plush as those in the Cooper S, but are well appointed considering the $16,850 price. *MINI USA*

Center-mounted twin tailpipes and aggressive lower rear fascia are a tip-off that you were just passed by the high-strung Cooper S. *MINI USA*

Besides the supercharged, intercooled 163-horsepower 1.6-liter engine, Getrag six-speed manual transmission, sport suspension plus, and traction control, the Cooper S offers a number of standard equipment items that are unique in terms of its exterior and interior versus the MINI Cooper. The exterior details include a functional hood (bonnet) air scoop, aggressive-looking body-color front and rear bumpers, a rear spoiler, twin center-exit chrome-plated tailpipes, front fender-mounted side grilles with integrated 'S' logo, a body-colored radiator grille, black-colored lower side sills and wider fender flares, and a chrome-plated quick-release fuel tank filler cap. Also standard are 16-inch alloy wheels finished in either white or sil-

Among early MINI buyers, the optional checkerboard roof graphic lags behind the Union Jack and U.S. flag. Old Glory is ahead of the Union Jack by a slight margin in the U.S.

ver with 195/55 R-16 run-flat all-season tires. In addition to the eight exterior colors offered on the MINI Cooper, the Cooper S can also be ordered in two exclusive "S" colors: Electric Blue Metallic or Dark Silver Metallic.

On the inside, the Cooper S distinguishes itself with standard leather sport seats, a leather-wrapped steering wheel and gearshift handle, stainless steel driver's footrest, and alloy patina door and fascia trim.

The MINI Cooper officially hit the racetrack in the U.S. in a special Mini race sanctioned by the SCCA at Laguna Seca Raceway in November 2001. Fifty-two Minis turned up for the race, ranging from highly modified national championship–caliber cars to vintage racers. The Mini Mania MINI qualified 12th and finished 7th. *Mitch Rossi*

Chapter Seven

WHAT'S NEXT?
MINIS of the Future

The arrival of the new MINI Cooper in America is only the beginning of a story that should see the same enthusiasm for aftermarket accessories and performance parts that the old Mini inspired. As for future production models, BMW has plans for the further evolution of its premium small-car lineup.

The Racing MINI

Almost five months before BMW officially let the new MINI Cooper loose on the streets of America, one of the Mini Cooper's U.K. siblings had already done battle on one of this country's premier racetracks. Northern California's Mini Mania has been in the business of developing and selling high-performance Mini parts and accessories since 1975. It was only natural that they get involved with setting up the first new MINI Cooper racecar in the United States.

Mini Mania's Don Racine had managed to get permission to import a U.K.-spec MINI Cooper for one year to use as a test mule for developing racing parts and accessories. At the end of the year the car could no longer remain in the United States. It would have to be sold outside the country. Expect it to show up in either Canada or Mexico.

Racine's plan was to spend about $100,000 and three to six months getting the car ready for a special Mini race to be held under the auspices of the SCCA at Laguna Seca Raceway in November 2001. About 50 classic Mini racecars were expected to be competing in the race.

Unfortunately, by the time he cut through all the red tape and the MINI Cooper arrived at Racine's shop in Nevada City, California, there were only six weeks to go before race day. Racine

and his crew were determined to make the race and set about modifying the areas that they felt needed the most work for better on-track performance. The stock suspension was deemed too soft for serious competition work. They also wanted the capability to adjust settings based on driver preference. The stock MINI Cooper springs are rated at 160 pounds, Mini Mania went to 300-pound units up front and 200 pounds for the rear. Fully adjustable Koni shocks were also part of the modifications.

The front strut upper locating mounts were redesigned to allow the mechanic to dial in as much as 2 degrees of negative camber. A strut

In addition to the usual safety equipment, the U.K.-spec, Mini Mania MINI was fitted with heavier springs front and rear, a front strut brace, and larger brakes. A cat-back exhaust was also added. The idea was for Mini Mania to use the car as a rolling test lab to develop parts and accessories. *Mitch Rossi*

Mini Mania was forced by regulation to sell its non-U.S.-spec car after one year. It had to leave the country. Mini Mania is developing a line of performance products that will fit U.S.-spec cars. *Mitch Rossi*

brace tied together the upper front shock mount towers to stiffen up the chassis. The stock front anti-roll bar was left in place.

The changes to the rear suspension provided what Racine considers to be the most dramatic improvements to the MINI Cooper's handling. A beefier 20-mm bar that is also adjustable replaced the stock 16-mm rear anti-roll bar. To better control both rear camber and toe, the non-adjustable stock control link arms were replaced with heavy-duty, Heim-jointed links. The rear of the car was also lowered significantly.

The brakes were the next area slated for improvement. Up front, huge 13-inch Brembo rotors with four-puck calipers were adapted in place of the stock 10.9-inch discs. At the rear, the stock calipers were retained to maintain the balance in the braking system, but the rotors were replaced by slotted and vented units. Hoosier DOT-approved race tires, 205/40-17, were mounted on 7.0x17-inch BBS alloy wheels.

In the engine compartment, improvements were limited to a high-flow exhaust manifold and cat-back exhaust system as well as some chip tuning of the ECU for better response in the racing power band. In all, horsepower is estimated to have been improved by about 10 percent.

Other modifications included the installation of a body kit to enhance aerodynamics and stripping of the interior to lighten the car. For safety purposes, a roll cage, safety harnesses, and a pair of MOMO race seats were added.

On race day, the Mini Mania MINI Cooper took to the grid along with 51 classic Minis, including three full-race national championship–caliber cars. Racine qualified 12th on the grid and by the end of the race had moved up to finish a respectable 7th behind cars that benefited from more modifications and development time than his car.

Their first racecar experiment may be over, but Mini Mania continues with the development of go-faster products for the MINI Cooper including an oil cooler kit, short shifter, close-ratio gear set, a performance clutch, various suspension modifications, the cat-back exhaust, a limited-slip differential, a freer-flowing cylinder head, and a turbocharger kit they think will produce 170 horsepower.

Street Performance

Like its predecessor, the new MINI seems to respond enthusiastically to a bit of aftermarket tinkering. At least that is the impression after driving one of the first cars to expand on the stock offerings from MINI USA.

Special Vehicle Concepts of Newport Beach, California, initially established itself as a high-quality aftermarket tuner by working magic on another British icon, the Land Rover. Over the last half-dozen years, Peter Cameron's SVC has expanded to cover a broad range of vehicles, primarily SUVs. The Cameron SSE MINI Cooper S illustrates a capability to understand small-car performance as well.

The stock MINI Cooper S is a pretty impressive performer out of the box, but SVC has intelligently selected and combined a short list of components to come up with a vehicle that shows a marked improvement in performance, handling, and appearance. More than one observer commented that the SVC Cooper S was the best-looking MINI that they had seen. A big part of the overall impression has to be the 18-inch Bezel wheels and Toyo 255/40-18 all-weather tires. SVC uses the factory aero kit pieces but subtly modifies the front and rear lower fascia and then adds distinctive shiny black paint trim.

The larger wheels and tires also make a significant improvement to the car's handling, as do the Eibach coil springs and anti-sway bars, which

Opposite, top: One of the first tuners to tackle the Cooper S in the U.S. was Peter Cameron of Special Vehicle Concepts in Newport Beach, California. The Cameron SSE MINI Cooper S looks and performs stunningly well thanks to 18-inch Bezel wheels and Toyo 255/40R-18 tires. Eibach springs and anti-sway bars take the handling of the stock S to the next level.

Opposite, bottom: A Magna-Flow cat-back exhaust adds 18 horsepower and a throaty growl. The total package, including aero kit and paint, adds about $10,000 to the Cooper S price. A larger brake kit is the next modification in the works.

New MINI Concepts

The original Mini had 133 different iterations during its life span, so it is no surprise that BMW is already working on a number of MINI concept cars. Most likely, the next model to next hit the streets will be a cabriolet, probably in late 2003 or 2004. *MINI USA*

eliminate the stock car's tendency to lean a bit more than is desirable, especially in tight corners.

A Magna-flow cat-back exhaust system adds a distinctive growl while adding a bit more low-end torque for smoother throttle response at low rpms. Cameron backs up this seat-of-the–pants sensation with a dyno sheet that shows his Cooper S has 18 more horsepower at the front wheels (158 versus 139.9) than the stock car. A fatter torque curve starts out with about 10 more ft-lbs at 2,000 rpm than stock and ends up at 141.2 ft-lbs versus 125.7 around the 6,500 rpm mark.

None of this comes cheap, with all of the above modifications performed by SVC for about $9,500, not including the price of a stock Cooper S. Then again, it is a far better deal than the thousands of dollars of markup for pinstriping, stain-proofing of upholstery, and other "dealer prep" items that some greedy MINI dealers, taking advantage of

MINI supply and demand, are adding to the sticker prices of the MINIs on hand in their showrooms for immediate delivery.

Future MINIs

BMW prefers to let the current wave of MINI madness run its course before trumpeting new models and variations. Jack Pitney of MINI USA, however, has said that the MINI is a brand and not just a limited model range.

"We aren't just introducing the MINI Cooper and Cooper S, we're introducing the MINI Cooper brand. That means that ultimately the brand has to produce its own self-grown product."

Pitney did not make any specific commitments, but he obviously had intentions of using the original Mini for inspiration regarding the MINI brand's potential future models.

"A convertible, station wagon, Mini Mokes, a dump truck," he conjectured. "There are so many different directions that we can take this brand."

Most pundits think a convertible MINI will be next. So far, BMW's only revelation regarding future models has involved another direction that the MINI may take. At the 2001 Frankfurt auto show, BMW revealed the hydrogen-powered MINI. The company has already backed up its faith in hydrogen power as a way to eliminate harmful emissions, with a special fleet of 7-series

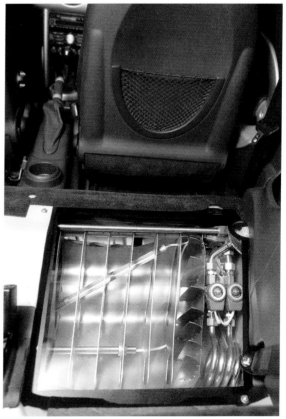

Top: A hydrogen-powered MINI was unveiled at the 2001 Frankfurt auto show. This "green" MINI follows in the tracks of the fleet of hydrogen-fueled 7-series cars that BMW has been testing for the last two years.

Right: Ultra-cold liquid hydrogen is stored in a fuel tank under the floor behind the front seats. The 1.6-liter Pentagon gasoline engine has been converted to run on hydrogen. *MINI USA*

The biggest problem regarding the feasibility of hydrogen power is the lack of a fuel distribution infrastructure for the average consumer. The hydrogen-powered MINI is shown here filling up at a station in the Munich airport. *MINI USA*

luxury sedans that has been undergoing road testing in a number of different locations over the last two years. The MINI Hydrogen Concept car takes that technology to the small-car market. The hydrogen-powered MINI uses the 1.6-liter four-cylinder engine from the gas-powered model, converted to run on ultra-cold liquid hydrogen. Before this MINI hits the showrooms, a number of details must be worked out regarding the infrastructure needed for public distribution of liquid hydrogen as a readily available alternative to gasoline or diesel fuel.

INDEX

**Porsche 911 Red Book
1965-1999**
ISBN 0-76903-0723-7
129810

**How to Restore & Modify
Your Porsche 914 and 914-6**
ISBN 0-76903-0584-6
128078

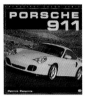

Porsche 911
ISBN 0-76903-0769-2
131724

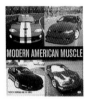

Modern American Muscle
ISBN 0-76903-0609-5
133358

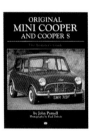

**Original Mini Cooper
and Cooper S**
ISBN 0-76903-1228-1
133838

Volkswagen Beetle
ISBN 0-76903-1078-5
134806

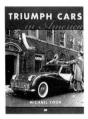

Triumph Cars in America
ISBN 0-76903-0165-4
125492

MG Sports Cars
ISBN 0-76903-0112-3
122884

BMW Buyer's Guide
ISBN 0-76903-1099-8
135105